The Young Country Doctor Book 11
Bilbury Delights

Vernon Coleman

Another collection of memories of Bilbury and its inhabitants.

Copyright Vernon Coleman 2017
The right of Vernon Coleman to be identified as the author of this work has been asserted in accordance with the Copyright, Designs and Patents Act 1988. Enquiries should be addressed to the author.

Note: Names and details of individuals, animals and establishments have been altered to protect the innocent, the guilty and the somewhere in-between.

The Author
Vernon Coleman is a *Sunday Times* bestselling author. He has written over 100 books which have been translated into 25 languages and sold in over 50 countries. His books have sold over two million copies in the UK alone. Vernon Coleman is also a qualified doctor. He lives in Bilbury, Devon, England. He is an accomplished bar billiards player (twice runner up in the Duck and Puddle Christmas competition) and a skilled maker of paper aeroplanes. He is a long-term member of the Desperate Dan Pie-Eater's Club (vegetarian section). He does not speak any foreign languages and cannot knit.

The Young Country Doctor series
This is the 11th book in the series. All the books in the series are available as ebooks on Amazon.

Dedication

To Antoinette, for whom my heart beats.

Foreword

It is one certainty that everything changes in life and another certainty that much of what is classed as progress is, in reality, nothing of the sort. Dodgem cars move around a good deal but they never actually get anywhere.

A third, and less widely appreciated, certainty is that in Bilbury things change so slowly that the changes are hardly noticeable.

In the last few years, for example, the only really big change I can think of is that (on my advice and under his wife's management) Frank Parsons of the Duck and Puddle has lost some weight and Peter Marshall has, for absolutely no discernible reason, moved the sardines from a shelf on the left of the shop as you enter to a shelf on the right. He has also moved the tinned rice pudding from the front of the shop to the back.

These are the sort of changes I can live with.

It is a constant delight to know that many other people around the world share our joy in the knowledge that there is still at least one village remaining where old-fashioned concepts such as honour, integrity, responsibility, tolerance, dignity, compassion, loyalty, respect (both for oneself and for others) and kindness are as much a part of daily life as the rain and the winds which regularly scour the North Devon coastline.

It is my belief that kindness (offered for its own sake rather than in the hope of reward or glorification) is the most fundamental and important human quality. It is the source of all other good qualities.

Like people everywhere, the villagers who live in Bilbury are sometimes bullied by Fate and tossed from one misfortune to another. They are, inevitably, exposed to their fair share of disappointments and frustrations. Nevertheless, to a man and a woman, they never become soured or vindictive or evil-minded. There is a decency about the citizens of Bilbury which transcends all else.

It is a comfort to know that such decency still exists in a world where intolerance, spite and selfishness are all too often regarded as inevitable and commonplace.

The stories in this book, and the others in this series, are as always all set in the 1970s but Bilbury today has not changed one whit.

Physically, the village is virtually the same as it was back in the 1970s.

The lanes are still narrow and, in the summer, they are overgrown so much that it is impossible to drive a car along them without scratching the paintwork on both sides.

The trees and hedges are notably higher than they were back in the 1970s, and the houses and cottages a little more weather-beaten.

But that's about it.

For this, we can probably thank the fact that our village is too small and too far off the beaten track to have attracted developers or planning officials.

Most of those who have had Bilbury in their sights have got lost, given up and gone home long before they could do any lasting damage.

(I have to confess that the absence of road signs (itself no accident) has made it difficult to navigate the local lanes.)

On the rare occasions when development plans have materialised, the villagers have always found a way to protect their history, culture and environment. We in Bilbury can be a difficult lot when it comes to protecting our culture and our environment.

The village is also unchanged both culturally and spiritually, and for this we can thank the villagers themselves.

Bilbury is run for and by people who are kind, who do unto others as they would be done unto themselves and who have (on the whole) the saving grace of a good sense of humour.

Most important of all, I am pleased to report that the principal human individuals who appear regularly in these stories are still alive and reasonably well, though I have to admit that a few waistlines (including mine I'm sorry to say) are rather larger now than they were back in the 1970s. The consequences of too many good lunches at the Duck and Puddle are widely visible.

Frank Parsons, who has now reached an age where he feels he is entitled to be grumpy, is still fighting his appetite and his waistline and Gilly is still watching his alcohol consumption like a hawk. Thumper Robinson is still tickling trout and maintaining and mending machinery that should have been thrown onto the scrap heap a long while ago. Patchy Fogg is still hunting for rare and valuable antiques and selling items which are neither rare nor valuable. His customers are tourists who will hopefully never know that 'the desk at which Shakespeare sat while writing his plays' was knocked up in a shed in Torrington by an old carpenter, with a seemingly inexhaustible supply of old timber and a knack for making it look even older.

Patsy is as beautiful as ever and still the best cook in the world.

It is difficult to believe that it is over 40 years since the events in this book took place. I suppose those of us who were present should be grateful that we're still here!

In this collection of memories, I have included an account of two Americans, Alston and Esme Church, who came to Bilbury to visit Cedric, the pig who was won in a skittle competition by previous American visitors Edgar and Delphinium Rathbone.

'Yours is a community in the true sense of the word,' wrote Esme, when they had returned home. 'It was an inspiration to visit Bilbury. There is more kindness shown in your village than in any town or city we have ever visited.'

With Esme's permission, I pinned her letter up on the noticeboard which hangs in the porch of the Duck and Puddle. The letter is still there, weathered and sun-faded. Some time ago, Patsy put it into a small photo frame to give it some protection.

There is a P.S. at the bottom of her letter, and this often produces a smile on the faces of visitors.

'We will always have Bilbury,' she wrote, paraphrasing Rick in Casablanca.

Underneath the framed letter from Esme, a visitor has pinned up a postcard upon which they have written the words: 'Bilbury will live forever in our hearts.'

So say I.

It is a privilege to call Bilbury 'home'.

It can be your home too.

After all, as they say, home is where the heart is.

Vernon Coleman, Bilbury 2017

Cedric's Admirers

'Frank is on the phone,' said Patsy. 'He wants to know if you know anyone called Church?'

I racked the remains of my brain and thought hard. I couldn't think of anyone called Church. Bells were not ringing loudly. Patsy handed me the telephone.

'Do you have a first name available?' I asked Frank.

'Alston,' said Frank. 'He says his name is Alston Church. He's American. His wife is called Esme. They're sipping Martinis and munching their way through Gilly's 'Fromage Anglais sur Pain Blanc avec Deux Cornichons Marine et Un Oignon au Vinaigre'. They want to know where to find Bilbury Grange.'

The Duck and Puddle is constantly tinkering with its menu and trying to make its offerings sound intriguing and slightly continental. Fromage Anglais sur Pain Blanc is a massively thick sandwich (sometimes known colloquially as a 'doorstep') which is made with cheddar cheese and white bread and served with two pickled gherkins and a pickled onion. Frank has never mastered the French language (there are some who say, rather rudely, that he has never mastered the English language either) and you need to know the Duck and Puddle menu to be able to guess the dish he is describing.

'Do they look dangerous?' I asked.

'He's wearing plaid trousers and a lemon coloured blazer,' replied Frank. 'And Mrs Church has blonde hair and a lime green jacket with yellow piping. The hair is fluffed up like candyfloss and there seems to be quite a good deal of it.' He paused. 'I think that perhaps they might be foreign; maybe American.'

'So you don't think they look as if they are likely to be planning to shoot me or beat me over the head with an iron bar?'

These may sound odd questions. But there was a reason for them.

It's not unusual for readers of my books and columns to turn up in Bilbury. Most of these visitors are courteous, friendly and kind and simply want to take a photograph or to have a book signed. But there have been a few angry callers who have turned up looking for an argument. One man, a keen hunter, turned up carrying a shotgun and I had to spend an hour talking to him before he would agree not to shoot me. He disagreed strongly with my views about shooting wild animals and argued vehemently that anything which walked on four legs was, by his definition, vermin and fair game. Another angry visitor, a woman who had believed that Bilbury and its inhabitants were all figments of my imagination, had come to complain after losing five shillings in a bet with a friend. She carried a large, multi-coloured golf umbrella which she brandished as though it were a sword and she were Errol Flynn about to turn the Sheriff of Nottingham into a pincushion.

'Oh no, I wouldn't think it very likely,' said Frank with damp reassurance. 'Shall I ask them what they want?'

I said I thought that would be an excellent idea.

Frank put down the telephone and I could hear him talking to the visitors and asking them why they wanted to visit Bilbury Grange.

'They say they'd very much like to see how Cedric is doing,' said Frank, upon his return and the resumption of our conversation. 'They've brought him a large bag of bananas. They say they're friends of the Rathbones.'

'Cedric!' I exclaimed. 'Cedric the pig? They've come to see Cedric? That's wonderful.'

Cedric is a very friendly pig who lives in one of the outbuildings at Bilbury Grange and who loves having visitors.

'Who is Cedric and who are the Rathbones?' asked Frank, clearly puzzled.

'The night you had your stroke,' I reminded him, 'the Duck and Puddle was running a Bowling for a Pig competition. Cedric was the pig and the Rathbones were the lovely Americans who won him.'

The Rathbones hadn't been able to take Cedric back to Idaho with them and so they'd asked Patsy and me to look after him. We had suitable accommodation for him at Bilbury Grange and we had happily accepted Cedric as part of our extended family. Patsy regularly sent letters and photographs across the Atlantic to the Rathbones. The fact that the visitors knew that Cedric liked bananas was as good as a password. We had only discovered Cedric's penchant for this particular fruit fairly recently and Patsy had sent the Rathbones a picture of Cedric munching his way through two pounds of bananas – peel and all.

To be honest, I had always thought that pigs would eat anything without much preference but when we took on the responsibility of looking after Cedric, Mr Kennet, my father-in-law, explained to us that pigs are far fussier than most of us realise.

So, for example, pigs cannot safely eat meat or fish and they should avoid sugar-rich foods.

Most surprisingly, Mr Kennet told us that pigs can be made ill by eating parsnips, turnips, cabbage, broccoli or cauliflower, though he admitted that in small quantities the chances of there being any problems are slight.

Citrus fruits can upset pigs and so, sometimes, can potatoes.

The good news is that pigs are intelligent and sensible creatures, with a strong sense of self-preservation, and they won't usually eat anything which is likely to upset them.

'Oh, yes!' said Frank, as the light suddenly dawned and he remembered Cedric the pig and the skittle competition.

Frank's stroke had put him into our Bilbury hospital and his recovery had taken weeks. He had been seriously ill and I wasn't surprised that he didn't immediately remember the name of a pig who had been the prize in the pub's skittles competition, or the name of the people who had won him. 'I'll give them directions and send them along when they've finished their…'

'…cheese sandwiches,' I interrupted, to save Frank the problem of having to struggle once again with the mysteries of the French language.

'Exactly!' said Frank, clearly grateful.

Alston and Esme Church turned up less than half an hour later.

As advertised by Frank, Alston Church was wearing plaid trousers and a lemon yellow jacket and Esme, who was wearing a pale blue pleated skirt and a slightly fluorescent lime green jacket with yellow piping was the proud owner of a good deal of blonde hair which looked casually styled but which had, I rather suspected, taken a considerable amount of time to prepare.

The Churchs were driving a bright orange Saab which they later told us they had rented from a company at Heathrow Airport. They both seemed enormously friendly and likeable. Patsy and I took to them immediately. They were excited at having met Frank and Gilly. 'I felt I already knew them so well from your books,' said Esme, who seemed as full of energy and expectation as a child at a birthday party.

'While we were having lunch, a fellow called in for a pint of a beer called Old Restoration,' said Alston. 'He was tall and very broad and he was driving a huge and very battered truck which had what looked like steel girders strapped to the front and the back.'

'That would have been Thumper,' said Patsy. 'I don't think anyone else in the village drinks Old Restoration. It's a particularly potent brew. I once drank half a pint, just to see what it tasted like, and I was squiffy for a week afterwards!'

Esme and Alston looked at each other. 'I told you it was him!' said Esme, very pleased with herself.

They both seemed thrilled that they'd seen Thumper Robinson.

'He's much bigger than I'd expected!' said Esme. 'He's quite a giant!'

I promised to introduce them to Thumper and to Patchy before they left Bilbury.

'I've got some scones warming in the oven,' Patsy told them as soon as they arrived. 'Would you like tea, coffee, beer, home-made lemonade or a glass of wine?'

They both asked for home-made lemonade and asked if they could perhaps tackle the scones after visiting Cedric.

'I've never been served a sandwich as big as that one I was given at the Duck and Puddle!' drawled Alston. 'It must have had half a pound of cheese inside it! I couldn't eat more than half of it and even so I'll need to do a little serious digesting before I can tackle anything else in the food line.' He shook his head. 'Not like me not to be able to finish a good lunch. But my appetite has been down a little recently.'

'You're really Patsy?' said Esme, standing back and looking at my wife, as though assessing her. 'I've read all the books your husband has written about the village. I thought it was so sweet how you two first met. It seems extraordinary to be here talking to you and finding for sure that you're a real person.'

'I'm real!' said Patsy, with a big smile.

'Our friends, Edgar and Delphinium told us so much about Bilbury,' said Esme, 'but I couldn't believe that one day I'd actually be standing here in your lovely village. It's just as beautiful in real life as it sounds in your husband's books!'

'We were confused by the fact that we couldn't find anywhere called Bilbury on the map,' said Alston. 'We found a village called Bibury but that was miles away in Gloucestershire.'

'That's because I changed the name of the village when I wrote the first book,' I admitted. 'I thought the villagers might not be too pleased with me if I printed the real name of the village and the book then became popular. Besides, the General Medical Council doesn't take kindly to doctors advertising or promoting themselves.'

We showed them around the house and introduced them to Miss Johnson, the children and the cats. Ben, our ever-friendly dog, introduced herself, of course. (We had to remind them that Ben, despite her name, is a lady.)

As we walked around the garden, I apologised for the number of weeds.

'Naturam expellas furca, tamen usque recurret,' said Esme, who turned out to be a schoolteacher responsible for guiding teenage Americans through the intricacies of Latin and Greek.

I studied Latin at school but after a short struggle, I admitted defeat and asked Esme for the translation.

'Even though you drive out nature with a pitchfork, she will always return,' said Esme, explaining that the quotation originated with Horace, the Roman poet.

We all agreed that it was remarkably apt, and something of a comfort in a strange sort of way. Later on, Esme gave us a list of other wonderful quotations – suitable for all sorts of odd happenings. At my request, she wrote them down and the list appears as an appendix at the back of this book.

And then we took them to meet Cedric.

'My oh my!' said Esme, in astonishment. 'I've never seen a pig as big as that. How much does he weigh? Do you know? Do you have any idea?' She tentatively fed one of the bananas to Cedric. He ate it in seconds and happily looked up at her, clearly waiting for a second helping.

'They have weighing scales for lorries at the local garage,' I said, 'so I walked her round there one day. She weighs 232 pounds. Or at least she did a couple of months ago. I suspect she's put on a few pounds since then.'

Cedric, like all pigs, seems to have an insatiable appetite, and like P.G.Wodehouse's creation, Lord Emsworth, I find myself taking great pride in his size, though unlike his Lordship I draw the line at dragging Cedric from his sty to make an appearance in any of the local shows. Mind you, I have been tempted. The local branch of the Private Pig Breeders Association gives a magnificent silver plate cup to the owner of the largest pig in Devon. But I don't think Cedric would like being put on display. It's all a question of dignity, isn't it? Dignity and respect.

Esme and Alston continued feeding bananas to Cedric who munched his way through all that they'd brought as quickly as they were offered. It is no exaggeration to say that Cedric has a 'good appetite'.

'Did you say you walked him round to the weighing scales?' asked Alston, who sounded surprised.

'He likes going for a walk,' I told him. 'Once or twice a week we take him for a stroll through the village. Sometimes we take him down to the village shop and Peter gives him a few leftover vegetables.'

'That's Peter Marshall's shop?'

'It is indeed,' I agreed.

'And sometimes, as a special treat, we take her to the Duck and Puddle,' said Patsy. 'She is particularly fond of one or two of Gilly's cheese sandwiches.'

'But what sort of lead do you use?' asked Alston. 'You'd need a hell of a chain to hold a pig that size. And how do you hold him if he decides he wants to go another way.'

'He's as good as gold,' laughed Patsy.

'And this is his lead,' I told them, lifting up a long piece of ordinary string which I keep looped on a nail on the outside of her sty.

Alston and Esme stared at the string in astonishment.

'This is his collar', I added, picking up a vast leather collar which a friend of Frank's had made for us. 'He did have a ring in his nose but we had it taken out. It looked painful and certainly wasn't dignified.'

'You can really take him for a walk with that piece of string as a lead?'

'He doesn't really need a lead,' said Patsy. 'He enjoys going for a walk and he follows us everywhere we go. If he stops too long, nibbling something he's found by the wayside, we just give a gentle tug on the string and along he comes. But if we called him, he'd come without the string.'

'If anyone ever makes a film of your books, the story about Cedric will surely be one of the highlights!' said Esme.

'Maybe Cedric could get to play himself!' suggested Alston.

'I think he'd like that!' laughed Patsy. 'He loves getting lots of attention.'

After admiring Cedric, being astonished at the feebleness of his lead and taking an enormous number of photographs with a still camera and a short piece of film with a movie camera, Alston and Esme allowed us to lead them into the drawing room at Bilbury Grange. Patsy served home-made scones, which had been warmed in the Aga, together with bowls of rich, whipped cream from her father's cows and two varieties of home-made jam.

As they enjoyed Patsy's Devon cream tea, our American visitors told us that they were approaching the end of a tour which had taken them on a six week trip around Europe. They had begun their holiday in Paris, spent a few days in Germany, visited Italy, gone to Spain and spent a few days in each of Holland, Belgium and Switzerland.

'We kept the best to last,' said Esme. 'Visiting England was always going to be the highlight of our trip. And coming to Bilbury was very much the icing on the cake.' She told us that they were both feeling tired and that Alston, in particular, was feeling the effects of a long and arduous vacation. They had done some of their travelling by aeroplane and some of it by train but they had hired cars in several European countries and Alston had done all of the driving. 'My appetite has really gone south,' said Alston, rather apologetically. 'Not like me at all.'

'Still, I think you've lost a few pounds in the last week or ten days,' said Esme. 'And your doctor at home wanted you to lose a little weight.' I secretly agreed with Alston's doctor in America. Alston was not tall, probably no more than five foot eight, but he was a big man and if he'd been a cake in a weight guessing contest at a summer fete, I'd have guessed he probably weighed 180 pounds.

Alston said that although they had only been in Britain for less than a week, they had already learned two new things about the British.

'First,' he said, 'I am amazed at the length of time for which the British will hold a grudge. Don't get me wrong, I love Britain and I love the British but my, oh my, some people in your country know how to hold a grudge, don't they? I'm surprised that there aren't people in your country who still feel resentment at the Boston Tea Party and the American Revolution!'

Patsy and I both laughed. 'There probably are!' said Patsy.

'We stayed in a pub in a little village in the Cotswolds,' continued Alston, 'and while we were there, this fellow came into the bar for a drink. The trouble was that the barmaid refused to serve him. Apparently this happens every time he goes into the bar – which is in the only pub for miles around, so if the poor fellow wants a drink he doesn't have a whole lot of choices.'

'We thought that perhaps there was some personal history between the fellow who'd come in for a drink and the barmaid,' said Esme, taking up the story. 'You know, maybe they'd had a relationship which had ended badly.'

'But it wasn't that at all,' said Alston. 'The pub landlord came in from the pub's small dining room and he served the fellow his pint of mild and bitter.'

'We talked to the landlord later,' said Esme, 'and being a rather inquisitive sort of person I asked about the history between the barmaid and the customer she wouldn't serve. We were astonished when the landlord told us that the problem was family not personal and that it apparently went back over a century! Can you believe it?'

'The great great grandfather of the barmaid was once sold a horse which wasn't everything it was made out to be,' explained Alston. 'And the person who sold it to him was some long-dead, distant relative of the fellow who'd come in for a drink. Ever since, there had been a feud between the two families. They all lived in the same village but they wouldn't have anything to do with one another.'

'Some grudge, eh?' said Esme. 'I don't believe any other people hold grudges for so long. The Americans certainly don't. Not even the Sicilians can hold a grudge as tightly as the British.'

Patsy told them that she wasn't surprised and that she knew of similar feuds, vendettas and grudges in Devon. 'These things tend to go on in rural communities,' she explained. 'In towns and cities the people move away and feuds get forgotten. But in the countryside, a good grudge can last centuries. No one can really remember what the grudge is about, only that the Bagshaws and the Hetheringtons have always despised one other, still despise one another and will always despise one another.'

'Sometimes, young members of each family fall in love and get married and when that happens the wedding is usually something to avoid,' I added.

Esme seemed shocked at this. 'Surely they suspend their hostilities for the wedding ceremony? For the sake of the loving, young couple who are getting married.'

'I'm afraid not!' said Patsy. 'There was a wedding in South Molton six months ago and the two families involved had hated one another for longer than anyone could remember – though naturally no one could remember what the disagreement was about. At the reception afterwards there was a massive fight and 17 people were arrested.'

'Five of the people arrested were women, weren't they?' I said to Patsy. She nodded.

'Five or six of them,' she agreed.

Esme and Alston both looked shocked.

'What was the other thing you've learned?' I asked our American visitors.

'Oh, just that you British are so polite!' said Esme. 'We've never been to Britain before and no one warned us about it, but my you are so wonderfully polite!'

'Back home,' said Alston, 'someone who accidentally treads on your foot will usually apologise profusely. But in Stratford-upon-Avon I trod on a man's foot and he actually apologised to me.'

Patsy and I both laughed at this.

'If an Englishman is bitten by a dog he will apologise to the dog, the dog's owner and the ambulance crew that comes to take him to hospital,' agreed Patsy.

'Most sensible people who've been bitten by a dog would sue the dog's owner,' said Alston. 'But I get the feeling that in Britain, the person who has been bitten is likely to be sued for upsetting the dog and its owner by allowing himself to be bitten.'

We admitted that this wasn't too far from the truth.

Alston and Esme stayed with us for the evening.

Patsy cooked a meal, I opened a couple of bottles of claret which a grateful patient had given me, and we shared a splendid few hours.

They told us about their home in Ohio where Alston ran a garage with a convenience store attached to it and about their love of hiking and rafting. It was, they told us, while rafting on the Boise River in Idaho that they had met Edgar and Delphinium Rathbone, who had been friends of theirs for nearly 25 years.

'This was some years ago,' admitted Esme. 'These days we all stick to hiking.'

'And we tend to do that fairly slowly,' said Alston. 'I've had surgery on my knee and Edgar has had a hip replacement operation. So we don't push ourselves.'

It was nearly midnight when our two visitors drove back to the Duck and Puddle where they had booked a room for three days.

We didn't see the visitors on the following two days. They wanted to take a drive around North Devon and visit some of the other towns and villages in the area. They were quietly amused to discover that there really are places called Parracombe and Kentisbury as well as Combe Martin, Lynmouth and South Molton. They drove in to Barnstaple, so that they could take a look at Devon's biggest town and do a little shopping for souvenirs. Patsy had told them of several suitable and reasonably priced shops and had advised them not to miss the local market stalls.

It was an afternoon three days after we had entertained them at Bilbury Grange when we next heard from them.

I received a telephone call from Esme. She sounded anxious.

'I'm sorry to bother you,' she said. 'I hope you don't mind, but I'm afraid I need your medical expertise.'

She explained that Alston had woken up that morning feeling very weak and rather tired and had said that he'd spend the morning in bed, having a little rest. He said he just thought he was paying the price for a good deal of travelling. Esme had said that she would sit and write a final few postcards and spend an hour or so packing up her purchases to ensure that they didn't get damaged on the flight home.

But at lunchtime, Alston had been no better.

'He says he feels too weak to move,' said Esme, who sounded worried. 'He didn't have any breakfast and he hasn't eaten any lunch either. That's just not like him, doctor. Alston enjoys his food and he loves the meals here.'

She also told me that she'd taken his temperature and that he had a slight fever.

Less than ten minutes later, I was sitting beside their bed listening to Alston tell me that he'd never felt quite so weak and washed out.

Esme, clearly desperately worried, sat in a chair by the window.

'Have you passed any urine yet this morning?' I asked Alston.

The minute I'd sat down by the side of the bed I had decided on a provisional diagnosis. I had noticed that the sclera, the whites of Alston's eyes, had acquired a yellowish tinge. There had been no yellowing of the sclera when we'd met a few days earlier. I would have noticed.

'I had to get up at about six for that,' he said. 'But that's normal for me, these days. I usually wake about then to visit the bathroom. My doctor says my prostate is a little enlarged.'

'Did you notice anything odd about your urine?' I asked him. I didn't think his enlarged prostate had anything to do with his current health problem.

'It was very dark,' replied Alston immediately. 'The colour reminded me of that dark beer that comes from Ireland.'

'Guinness?'

'That's the one.'

'How long has your urine been dark?'

'A few days. Maybe a week. Yes, nearly a week. I think I first noticed it getting darker when we were in Amsterdam. That was also when I started to feel a bit tired. I put it down to too much travelling. We'd driven around 600 miles in two days. Do you think the colour change is significant? I assumed it was something I'd eaten. You know, in the way that urine goes red when you've been eating beetroot.'

'Have you had any other symptoms?'

'As I think I told you, I've been off my food a little. My appetite has gone and I've been feeling nauseous. I thought perhaps the nausea was putting me off my food but I don't know what's been causing the nausea. We came across the English Channel on the ferry and the sea was a little rough that day. I put the nausea down to a little sea sickness.'

'Have you had any abdominal pain?'

'Not really pain. Just a bit of discomfort.'

'How have your bowels been? Any change?'

'I've had a bit of diarrhoea,' said Alston, who seemed embarrassed.

'And the colour?'

'Colour?'

'The colour of your stools, your faeces?'

'Oh, that's strange because although my urine has definitely been darker my faeces have definitely been lighter. Clay coloured, I'd say.'

I pulled down the bedclothes and, having asked Alston to undo the cord of his pyjama trousers and to pull up his jacket, I examined his abdomen. I could find nothing of any note. I certainly couldn't find any sign of an enlarged liver.

'What do you think it is, doctor?' asked Esme.

I turned. She was sitting on the edge of her chair, twisting a handkerchief between her fingers.

I refastened the pyjama cord and rearranged Alston's bedclothes. 'I'm pretty sure you've got infective hepatitis,' I said, talking to Alston but also replying to Esme. I hate it when doctors talk about a patient as though he isn't there; discussing a diagnosis and treatment without addressing him directly.

'Oh my God!' cried Esme. She started crying.

I reassured them both that this probably sounded worse than it was. I explained that I felt sure that Alston had an infection of his liver, in particular a type of hepatitis known as 'infective hepatitis A', and that he had probably picked it up somewhere on their journey around Europe.

'It is not at all uncommon for travellers who've visited Paris to pick up hepatitis,' I explained. 'There seem to be a good many restaurants in the city where the kitchen staff are infected. And if hygiene isn't terribly good then the food they serve can be infected too.'

'We were in Paris about six weeks ago,' said Esme.

'That would fit perfectly,' I agreed. 'The incubation period is about six weeks – that's the usual sort of time interval between contracting the infection and showing symptoms.'

'But isn't hepatitis dangerous?' asked Esme.

'Some types can be quite nasty,' I agreed. 'But given all the circumstances I'm confident that Alston has a type of liver infection known as hepatitis A. And that's inconvenient and unpleasant rather than dangerous.'

'Should Alston be in hospital?' asked Esme.

Alston, lying back in bed looked exhausted and seemed happy for his wife to take over the questioning and the decisions.

'I think it would be a good idea,' I said. 'I'll take some blood samples which I'll send along to the laboratory in Barnstaple but I'm pretty confident about the diagnosis.

'Where's the nearest hospital?' asked Esme. 'What do you recommend? Should we take him up to London? We took out good health insurance for this trip. I'm sure our insurers will pay for the best treatment available.'

'It's up to the two of you,' I told them. 'If my diagnosis is correct then Alston simply needs nursing care. There isn't any treatment. Alston will slowly recover and the only important thing is to keep him comfortable and well hydrated. There's a hospital in Barnstaple and a private hospital in Exeter. And there are, of course, plenty of private hospitals in London.' I also explained that we had a small, cottage hospital in Bilbury.

'How long am I going to be ill?' asked Alston.

'A few weeks, possibly even a month or two,' I told him. 'There isn't any way to hurry up the recovery – other than to make sure that you rest and give your body a chance to deal with the infection.'

'Oh dear,' said Esme. 'When do you think Alston will be fit to travel back to the States?'

'Not until he feels a little better,' I told her. 'I wouldn't want him to make a long journey for a few weeks – probably a month at least. He needs to get his strength back and that will take time.'

I took out a syringe and needle and a couple of blood sample bottles. And I took samples of Alston's blood to send to the laboratory.

'How infectious is the disease?' asked Esme.

'It's fairly infectious,' I told her. 'We need to make sure that Alston is properly nursed in such a way that the infection doesn't spread to anyone else. It's called barrier nursing. It just means making sure that the bug which has affected Alston doesn't get a chance to affect anyone else.

'Is Esme going to get this?' asked Alston. 'We've been together all the time.'

'Have you had any symptoms at all?' I asked her. 'Any of the problems Alston has described?'

Esme shook her head.

'And your urine is a normal colour?'

'Oh yes.'

'Then I don't think you're going to get it,' I told her. 'I would have expected you to have shown symptoms or signs by now.'

I left Esme and Alston to discuss hospitals while I went downstairs to arrange for the blood samples I'd taken to be sent over to Barnstaple. A van from the hospital comes round every morning and brings test results and takes away samples but we'd missed it for the day and I didn't want to wait until the next morning's collection. Fortunately, Gilly was going into Barnstaple to do some shopping and she happily agreed to drop off the blood samples at the hospital laboratory.

'You're going to lose your guests a little early,' I told her and Frank. I explained that they should make sure that Alston's room was well cleaned without any delay. I knew that all the crockery and utensils that are used at the pub are cleaned in their dishwasher so that wasn't a problem. I told them to make sure that the bed sheets and pillowcases were all washed at a high temperature. 'And it's important to make sure that the toilet and bathroom are well cleaned. Wear rubber gloves when you do the cleaning and burn the gloves afterwards.'

When I went back upstairs, I found that Esme and Alston had decided that they would go to London where there was a large, private hospital which their insurance company recommended. I would have been happy for Alston to stay at our cottage hospital in Bilbury (and that's certainly where I would have preferred to stay myself) but to be honest, I was a little relieved at the choice they'd made. Barrier nursing a patient with infective hepatitis requires a lot of work and our small hospital doesn't have the staff for that sort of work – particularly since Alston would probably need to be kept in bed for a month or six weeks.

A private ambulance arrived two hours later and took Alston and Esme off to London. I promised to telephone the hospital with the results of the blood tests as soon as they were available, though I knew that the hospital in London would repeat the tests.

Esme telephoned us several times during the next month. The doctors in London confirmed my diagnosis and they kept Alston in hospital for just over four weeks. When they gave Alston the 'all clear' the couple flew back to America.

Happily, neither of them had bad feelings about Bilbury – despite the fact that it was in our village that Alston had been taken poorly.

Both insisted that their visit to see Cedric and the rest of us in the village had been the highpoint of their vacation. And Cedric's North American fan club has now doubled in size.

Alston and Esme were not, however, quite so fond of their trip to Paris.

The doctors in London had confirmed that the chances were that Paris was where Alston had acquired his unwelcome souvenir.

The good news was that Alston made a complete recovery and five months later he, Esme and our good friends the Rathbones sent us a postcard from another of their hiking adventures in the Rocky Mountains.

The Orang-utan

Al Packer works as an insurance salesman during the week but on Friday and Saturday evenings he turns himself into 'Darley Dale', a performer who appears in pubs and clubs throughout the West Country. He sings a mixture of traditional Devon folk songs (which he writes himself) and traditional country and western songs (which he also writes himself).

The traditional Devon folk songs are invariably rather sad and usually involve a young shepherd and his unrequited love for a farmer's daughter.

The country and western songs are about a cowboy who regrets the men he has shot and the cattle he has rustled.

In real life, neither Al nor 'Darley' has ever been further west than Bideford and I doubt if either of them has ever sat upon a horse. To be honest, I don't think Al knows anything much about horses. It is reputed that he once saw half a dozen llamas in a field on the way to Combe Martin and asked several people what sort of horse they were.

Al, who has never married, lives alone in a room which he rents from Samuel Houghton, a local farmer. To be honest, I don't think Al is a very good insurance salesman and I strongly suspect that he would give it up in a moment if he could earn enough money from his singing career.

'Darley' has a regular gig at a pub in Ilfracombe called The Dog and Two Ferrets. He appears there twice a month and the arrangement is that he receives a very small fee but is also allowed as much free beer as he can drink.

Sadly, the result of this (and similar arrangements at a pub in North Molton called The Nell Gwynn and a working men's club in Lynton called 'The Working Men's Club') 'Darley' (or should it be Al) has acquired a taste for alcoholic beverages which doesn't have much to do with thirst.

When I was a medical student, I was taught that the human liver removes alcohol from the bloodstream at a rate of around an ounce an hour and that, as a result, it is in theory perfectly possible to drink an ounce of alcohol every hour without ever showing any signs of being drunk.

The snag, of course, is that a steady consumption of alcohol means that the liver, which has the job of metabolising the stuff, tends to become rather worn out and bloated considerably sooner than might otherwise be the case.

And this, sadly, is what has happened to Al Packer's liver.

He came to see me complaining of nausea, continual tiredness, abdominal pain and swelling in his feet and ankles. His skin and eyes had a yellowish tinge. As a result of the blood tests I'd ordered and received, I'd had no choice but to read him the general practitioner's equivalent of the riot act. I pointed out to him that he was without doubt a fully-fledged alcoholic and that if he didn't change his ways then his future wouldn't be a very long one.

I told him to return to the surgery once a week so that I could keep an eye on his progress by repeating the blood tests.

Whenever he arrived for his check-up, he had obviously been chewing sweets which I recognised as Palma Violets. However, the sweet aroma of the traditional English delicacy failed entirely to mask the smell of the alcohol.

I must say, though, that although his face was always a little flushed, there were no other overt signs that he had been drinking; he did not seem to be in any way dangerously over-lubricated. Like a lot of heavy drinkers, he managed to give the impression of sobriety even when he had drunk enough alcohol to turn any normal person into a wobbly wreck.

The big problem was that Al had not yet accepted that his drinking was damaging his body. Indeed, on the contrary, he was convinced that a few drinks helped him perform much better when he was working as 'Darley'.

Lots of drinkers, particularly motorists, claim that their drinking makes them more confident and less hesitant.

Generally speaking, I've always found this argument to be rather specious and self-serving. It is, for example, well known that although motorists always think they drive better after a couple of drinks, their skills and judgement are invariably worse than they would have been if they had been sober. Alcohol increases confidence but reduces performance.

On the other hand, is the consumption of alcohol one of those areas of life where it is possible to separate the black from the white?

Maybe not.

I worked with two heart surgeons during one of my hospital jobs as a house surgeon and although they worked in the same department, and both did the same sort of operations on the same sort of patients, they were completely different characters.

One of the two surgeons, the younger, was very slow, very methodical and very cautious. If he had owned a powerful motor car he would have been the driver settled in the slow lane, following pantechnicons and fourteen wheelers at 40 mph. If he'd been a house painter he would have taken three weeks to paint a modest sized house but he would have done a perfect job and there wouldn't have been a drop of paint spilt anywhere. He was very straight-laced and liked everyone to call him 'sir'.

The other surgeon, the older of the two, was very fast but rather slapdash and if he had been a house painter there would have been paint on the windows, on the carpets and on the wrong bits of wall. He would have taken less than a week to complete the job and another day to clean up the mess he'd made. He was great fun and liked everyone he worked with, even or perhaps especially the junior nurses, to call him by his Christian name. His one big flaw was that he was rather excitable.

When I first started to work for him, the surgical registrar told me to 'watch his hands'.

'To learn?' I said, naively. 'Is he very good?'

'He is good,' said the registrar, 'but you need to watch his hands because if things aren't going well he has a tendency to throw things – including scalpels.'

While working with that surgeon, and standing on the other side of the operating table, I became very good at dodging knives.

The older surgeon lived in a massive old country house with a pool, a miniature golf course and its own maze. (He did a good deal of private work and made a lot of money from work at a local private hospital.) I remember that one Christmas, a group of us took his car apart and then reassembled it at the centre of his maze. He had to get a crane to lift it out of the maze but he thought it was a hysterically funny jape. I've never known anyone else who had their own maze. I've known several people who had their own boating lakes and two who had their own golf courses but only one who had his own maze. The hedges of the maze were made of leylandii which he had used because it is the fastest growing hedge material known to man. The snag, of course, was that a gardener had to trim the hedge once every few weeks during the summer. It was, I suspect, like painting and repainting the Forth Bridge.

Now, with surgeons, as with most professionals in most areas of life, the best way to measure skill is to match the success rate of one with another. And the ultimate way to measure the skill of surgeons is to measure the percentage of patients who leave the hospital alive and well and compare it with the percentage who leave the hospital encased in a wooden box. The only real way to judge a surgeon's skill is to measure his success rate when compared to colleagues performing similar operations on a similar group of patients.

You might have thought that of the two surgeons I've mentioned, the slow, methodical surgeon would have had the better success rate but you would have been wrong.

The fast surgeon, the one who attacked his patients as though he were tackling the undergrowth in an overgrown garden, wielding his scalpel with gusto, had a far better success rate. His patients were far more likely to live and more likely to get better quickly. The scar he left them with wasn't always neat but they lived. Knowledgeable GPs in the area usually sent him their patients. Even among the public it was quite widely known that he was the man to go to if you needed to go under the knife.

On the other hand, the patients who had been operated on by the slow surgeon had very neat scars, the sort that fade to a thin almost indiscernible white line, but too many of them did not live to parade their scars upon the beach.

There was a simple reason for this.

When a patient is on the operating table they are, inevitably, under an anaesthetic of some kind and their bodies are subjected to a whole series of abnormal physical insults. The risk of a patient faring badly, and developing complications or dying, depends to a very considerable extent upon the length of time an operation takes.

If one surgeon routinely completes his work in two hours and another surgeon takes four hours for the same operation then, all things being equal, the surgeon who completes his operations in the shorter time will have by far the better success rate. His patients will make a quicker recovery and they will be more likely to survive.

I was in the hospital mess when the slow and methodical surgeon, aware of the fact that too many of his patients were dying, asked his older colleague what he thought he could do to improve his success rate.

I knew that the careful surgeon was in a bad way; even talking of giving up surgery completely and retraining as a pathologist. His argument was that if he did post-mortems for a living then at least his patients would be dead when he began work on them. At the time, five of his last six patients had died on the operating table and the sixth was still seriously ill in the Intensive Care Unit.

That is a heavy burden to carry with you when you next scrub up and approach an unconscious patient lying on your operating table.

'Ah that's easy,' said the fast surgeon with a laugh. 'You're a damned good surgeon but you're far too uptight. You fuss too much, you're too nervous and you take too long over your cutting and stitching. Because you're too methodical and slow, your patients are under the anaesthetic for too long. You need to speed things up a bit.'

'But what can I do about it?' asked the methodical surgeon. 'I'm just a naturally cautious sort of fellow,' he added unnecessarily.

'Have a drink before you start work. Not enough to make you drunk, of course; but enough to get rid of some of your inhibitions; a glass of something to loosen you up a little.'

And so the slow surgeon started having a modest sized glass of port before he put on his operating mask and gown. The nurses and other staff were scandalised for the surgeon made no secret of his new habit. He kept a bottle of good port and an appropriate crystal drinking glass in his locker. I don't know why he chose port. I think he was probably nervous about drinking spirits because of the higher alcohol content.

But what is it that they say about the proof of the pudding?

And the fact is that the glass of port did its job.

The young surgeon's operations didn't take quite as long and his patients started to do well. Most important of all they survived.

As long as I was working for him, the surgeon never exceeded his one glass of port. And everyone, doubtless not least the patients and their relatives, was delighted that his terrible run of failure came to an end. No one who worked with him complained. Everyone was relieved.

And what difference does it make whether you relax a little by taking a pill or by taking a single glass of alcohol?

However, there is no doubt that not all those who drink are able to control their drinking so precisely.

Alcohol is an addictive substance and many heavy drinkers only discover that they have lost control when it is far too late.

I had absolutely no doubt that Al Packer was no longer in control of his drinking. On the contrary, the drinking was clearly in charge of him.

'Maybe I should just cut down my drinking,' suggested Al on one of his visits to the surgery. 'I could easily do that.'

'No!' I told him firmly. 'You need to cut out alcohol completely. You need to talk to a specialist and you need to join Alcoholics Anonymous.' I gave him the telephone number for Alcoholics Anonymous and explained how they could help him.

Al eventually left my surgery promising that he would keep the appointment I had made for him at a specialist clinic in Exeter.

I was not confident that he would attend the clinic. In my experience, alcoholics only start on the road to recovery when they acknowledge that they need help – and ask for it.

And so I felt rather gloomy when I set out on my morning rounds later that day.

I like Al Packer.

Some folk would undoubtedly regard him as a rather odd fellow but the word 'odd' can be used as a synonym for 'unusual' or 'fascinating' and I don't for a moment think that the world is a worse place for having a generous sprinkling of 'odd' folk around.

My calls that day took me from one end of the village to the other and as I was driving along the lane which leads past the Duck and Puddle, I went by the cottage belonging to Olive Robinson, Thumper Robinson's aunt. As I drove along, my eye was caught by a figure sitting on a wooden kitchen chair just a few feet from the edge of the roadway. I slowed down to a fast walking pace, because it seemed that the chair was dangerously close to the lane, and to my astonishment saw that the figure sitting on the chair was far too orange and hairy to be human: indeed, it wasn't a human at all. It was an orang-utan.

And it waved to me.

It waved to me!

I'd never seen an orang-utan before but I knew what this was just as surely as I would have recognised an elephant, a giraffe or a camel. I've seen plenty of pictures and there is no other creature in the world which can be mistaken for an orang-utan.

I was tempted to stop to find out why Miss Robinson had acquired a friendly orang-utan as a houseguest but I had one last call to do, to a Mr Rawlinson.

My receptionist, Miss Johnson, had stressed to me that it was important to arrive before lunchtime. I didn't know why the timing was so important but when Miss Johnson tells me something, I always listen and try to do what she suggests. I don't always understand why I am doing what I am doing but I have learned that she not only knows what she is doing but usually also knows what I should be doing.

Mr Rawlinson is a curious fellow. When I first met him, I assumed that he was in his 70s or 80s but in fact, he was only 52-years-old. He is, without a doubt, the laziest man I have ever met. His idea of exercise is turning on the television set in the morning and off again late at night. The muscles of his right forefinger and thumb must be especially well developed; honed within a fraction of an inch of muscular perfection.

Mr Rawlinson once told me that his main claim to fame lies with an ancestor of his called Thomas Rawlinson; an Englishman who invented the kilt back in the early 18th century.

The 18th century Rawlinson was an industrialist who reportedly invented the kilt because it was cheaper to make than a pair of trousers – and the Scots who worked for him were poor. He also thought the kilt was safer and easier to wear than the sort of complicated garments the workmen had previously favoured.

So he persuaded them to wear kilts – which were cheap and easy to manufacture.

However, about two decades later, in 1746, the British Parliament banned the kilt (in the 1746 Dress Act) because it was considered an embarrassment and too different to be acceptable form of attire. The

Highlanders had just been defeated at the Battle of Culloden and Parliament also wanted to make it clear who was in charge.

Before Parliament banned the kilt, it had been worn only by very poor workmen who couldn't afford to buy trousers. No laird would be seen dead in one. But, naturally, as soon as the kilt was banned, every contrary Scotsman wanted one. The richer and more Patriotic Scots definitely wanted the outlawed kilts. And because they had more money, they made the kilts more complicated – adding belts and pleats and so on. The sporran was added because the kilt had no pockets and there was nowhere for the Scotsman to put the 18th century equivalent of his mobile phone and car keys.

And so the kilt became the national costume of Scotland.

Bizarrely, each clan chief claimed that his tribe should wear a kilt with its own distinctive plaid pattern.

The myth about the kilt was carved into stone by Sir Walter Scott, the Scottish romantic author, who claimed that the kilt's history could be traced back to the third century.

This, of course, was imaginative nonsense.

For the kilt was invented in the 18th century by an Englishman called Rawlinson, whose descendant was now unbuttoning the top two buttons of a rather grubby flannel shirt.

Mr Rawlinson had asked for a home visit because he wanted me to listen to his chest.

'Do you have any breathing problems?' I asked.

'Oh no,' he replied, seemingly surprised by the question. 'I feel fine. I just want to make sure that I'm not about to fall ill. I can't afford to be poorly this week.'

'Ah!' I said, feigning wisdom. 'What's happening this week?' I thought that maybe he was about to tell me that he was having a job interview.

'It's the Cheltenham Festival,' he replied.

'Horse jumping?'

'That's right. It starts this afternoon and it's on all week.'

'You're off to Cheltenham?'

'No, no. I'm going to watch it on the television.'

And that, I realised, explained why Mr Rawlinson had told Miss Johnson that it was important that I visited him before lunch.

I listened to his chest, confirmed that all was well and assured him that he was fit enough to sit and watch the horse racing for the rest of the week. He seemed enormously relieved.

Outside his cottage, I stood for a moment and admired the acheiropoietoi which stands on the hill behind his garden.

An acheiropoietoi is, of course, a pictorial image which was not made by human hand and there are many of them in our part of North Devon. This particular acheiropoietoi is a stone which, thanks to a freak of nature, looks like a huge dog.

I have no doubt that not having motor cars, telephones or televisions to complicate their lives meant that the Greeks had plenty of time to wander around the countryside spotting bits of nature masquerading as old men, barking dogs or shapely young women.

And so that is why they had a name for this particular art form. They probably had special acheiropoietoi clubs and weekend acheiropoietoi festivals.

Anyway, the acheiropoietoi behind Mr Rawlinson's cottage is one of the best in our part of the world and certainly the best in Bilbury.

When I had finished admiring the stone dog, I drove away from Mr Rawlinson's home, and headed back towards Bilbury Grange.

The lanes in our village are usually quiet and I can often drive around for an hour or more without seeing any other traffic.

But half a mile away from home, I saw Thumper's truck approaching.

Now, the lanes in Bilbury are narrow and there isn't often enough room for two vehicles to pass each other. Most of the lanes are no more than seven or eight feet wide and because vehicles are restricted to travelling along the tracks made by other vehicles, the lanes have grass growing in the middle. This particular lane, which doesn't have a name, is, however, wide enough for two cars to pass if the drivers are cautious and don't mind tangling their nearside wing mirrors in the hedgerows either side of the road.

Thumper's truck looks as if it has been in a 15 round fight with a couple of large bulldozers and Thumper, who never worried about acquiring new dents and scratches, moved in a little so that his vehicle would rub along the hedge, leaving the Rolls a couple of inches of space to spare its paintwork. We both slowed to walking pace.

As our vehicles approached each other, I noticed that there was a passenger sitting in the front seat of Thumper's truck.

And as we got closer and closer I could see that the passenger was an orange-utan.

It seemed a fair bet that it was the same animal which had been sitting on a chair outside Miss Robinson's cottage.

And once again, the orang-utan was waving.

It was definitely, without a doubt, waving to me.

A long, reddish brown arm was raised in an impromptu salute and the animal was, without a doubt, waving in my direction.

It is always difficult to see precisely what is going on inside Thumper's truck because the windows are thick with several years' worth of accumulated grime and mud. I don't think Thumper has ever washed his truck. He has most certainly never subjected it to a polish.

But I could definitely see that the orang-utan was staring in my direction. And I could definitely tell that it appeared to be pleased to see me.

I blinked and looked again. The orang-utan was still there. If I had been to the Duck and Puddle I would have feared that I must have had too much to drink. Moreover, as a final, bizarre touch, the animal was clearly wearing its seatbelt.

As our vehicles came alongside, I brought the Rolls to a halt and looked across into the front of Thumper's truck. Thumper slowed and he too stopped.

I wound down my window. The orang-utan now began to wave with even greater enthusiasm – as though it had recognised me and was pleased to see me.

'Where...' I shouted, intending to ask Thumper where he had found an orang-utan. But I stopped myself. It seemed an inadequate question. What do you say to someone who is driving around with an orang-utan in the front passenger seat? 'Why have you got an orang-utan with you?' 'Where did you find that animal?' 'Is it dangerous?'

Thumper grinned across at me and rubbed the orang-utan's head with his left hand. The animal seemed to like this a good deal. Its head bobbed up and down and it moved across to be closer to Thumper.

'Wind down your window!' I shouted.

Thumper wound down his window.

'Is that what it appears to be?' I managed at last.

'It's an orang-utan,' replied Thumper with a big grin.

'I saw it a little earlier sitting outside your aunt's cottage.'

'I'm taking it for a ride,' explained Thumper. 'Showing it the neighbourhood.'

I stared at him and then at the orang-utan.

And then I noticed the piece of orange baler twine which was attached to the orang-utan's wrist. The baler twine merged into the creature's fur and was almost invisible.

Thumper saw me notice the string and, unable to contain himself any longer, he started to laugh.

'It's a stuffed toy!' I shouted.

'Took you long enough!' cried another voice, and Patchy Fogg suddenly appeared from his hiding place on the floor at the back of the truck. Patchy, I noticed, was holding the other end of the piece of baler twine which was tied to the creature's wrist.

'Patchy bought a job lot at an auction in South Molton,' explained Thumper. 'As part of the lot there was a large trunk filled with stuffed toys. This one is life-size.'

'You fooled me,' I admitted.

'We could have fooled anyone with it,' said Patchy with a laugh. 'We strapped it into the front seat with the seatbelt and tied bits of string to both arms so that I can sit in the back and make it wave to people.' He pulled at the two strings and the orang-utan raised both arms. It really did look very convincing.

I congratulated them both on the best practical joke I'd seen for months and then drove back to Bilbury Grange for my luncheon.

I'd finished eating and was sitting having my coffee when the doorbell rang. I put down my coffee but hadn't moved out of the chair when the doorbell rang again. It rang another four or five times before I got to the door.

'Someone is very impatient!' shouted Patsy from the kitchen. 'Who is it?'

It was Al Packer. He looked terrified. His yellowing skin was now deathly pale. He was sweating and seemed close to hysterics.

'Do you have the details of that appointment?' he asked me. 'The appointment with the hospital specialist? And have you got the phone number for Alcoholics Anonymous? I lost the piece of paper you gave me before.'

I knew he had probably thrown the paper away but I took him into the surgery, found the details he had requested and wrote them down for him again.

'I need help,' said Al. 'And I need it now.'

'What's changed your mind?' I asked him, pleased that he'd seen the light.

'I was just driving through the village when I saw Thumper in his van,' said Al. 'He had a big orange ape with him. And I swear the ape waved to me.'

'An orang-utan?' I asked.

'Yes, that's it,' said Al. 'Have you seen it?'

'An orang-utan in Thumper's van?'

'Yes. I saw it. The damned thing waved to me.'

'It doesn't seem very likely,' I said.

'No,' said Al. 'It doesn't does it? That's why I know I must have been having a hallucination. It's a sign that I need help.'

'You'll keep that appointment and you'll ring Alcoholics Anonymous?'

'Oh yes,' replied Al. 'I certainly will. You don't have to worry about that, doctor.'

Al left clutching the piece of paper I'd given him.

It takes on average 15 years to convince an alcoholic to put up a hand, admit they have a problem and ask for help.

For Al, the orang-utan in Thumper's truck speeded up the process considerably.

When he'd gone, I telephoned Thumper who had just arrived home for his standard 5,000 calorie midday meal.

'Does anyone else know about your jape?' I asked him.

'We only saw you and Al Packer,' said Thumper. He sounded rather disappointed.

'Do me a favour,' I said. 'Don't tell anyone else about the orang-utan. And put the damned thing away for a while.'

'That's a lot to ask,' said Thumper, sounding disappointed.

'I know it is. But it's in a good cause.'

There was a short silence. 'Ah,' said Thumper, seeing the light. 'Al thought he was having hallucinations, didn't he?'

I didn't say anything. I take patient confidentiality very seriously though obviously I couldn't prevent Thumper reaching the truth by himself.

'Got it,' said Thumper. 'If we drive around with the orang-utan, Al will know that it's a stuffed toy, realise that he wasn't having hallucinations and decide he doesn't need to ask for help.'

Once again, I didn't say anything.

'No problem at all,' said Thumper. 'I'll have a word with Patchy.' I could almost feel him wink at me. Thumper, like most people in the village, is fond of Al but knows that his drinking is out of control and he desperately needs help.

'Thanks,' I said.

'It turned out to be an ever better jape than we thought,' said Thumper, justifiably sounding rather pleased with himself.

And he was right.

You don't often come across a practical joke that does someone a good turn.

The Birthday Girl

Since I had taken over my medical practice in Bilbury, I had got into the habit of regularly visiting all my elderly patients, whether they were ill or not.

I had far more elderly patients than might have been expected from the size of the practice (there is, say the locals, something in the sea air that encourages good health and longevity) but even so, I could visit all my elderly patients on a regular basis simply by calling in on two or three most days.

If I was passing the home of a patient I hadn't seen for a few weeks, I would call in just to make sure that all was well.

I always had a supply of drugs in a locked bag in the boot of the Rolls, and if a patient was running out of a medicine they took regularly then I could provide them with additional supplies. Since Bilbury was some considerable distance from the nearest town, I had been granted the right to run what was called a 'dispensing practice'. This meant that I could keep supplies of drugs at Bilbury Grange – and locked in the boot of my car.

I was able to visit my elderly patients, even when they hadn't requested a visit, because I had a small practice and looked after no more than a quarter of the number of patients cared for by a doctor working in a large town or city.

It also helped that there wasn't anyone in the village who wasn't my responsibility.

I could be confident that behind every door I passed, the residents within were on my list of patients. And it was, of course, much easier for me to visit elderly, infirm patients than it was for them to visit me. We see charabancs in Bilbury from time to time but the last time I saw an ordinary bus driving round the lanes of Bilbury, it was only there because the driver, trying to get from Barnstaple to Lynton for the first time, had lost his way. Villagers who want to catch a bus must walk a considerable distance to a bus stop on the main road. There is no bus service within Bilbury itself.

My friend Will, who is a partner in a large practice in a town in the middle of England, has between 2,500 and 3,000 patients on his list. The numbers vary because in the town where he practices there is quite a good deal of movement among the population. People move into the town, or away from it, because they have married, taken jobs in the area or gone away to study at a university or college elsewhere.

In contrast, my practice in Bilbury consisted at the time of around 600 patients. There were sometimes one or two more, and there were sometimes one or two less, but the total didn't change very much.

The one big disadvantage of having such a small practice was that my income was considerably lower than that of a doctor working in a big city practice.

The National Health Service pays doctors a fee for each patient on their list and although I received some additional income from the NHS (including an extra fee because I looked after a small practice in a rural area) my total practice income was much lower than that of a city doctor with several thousand patients.

GPs working in towns and cities also have the opportunity to earn additional money by taking on extra jobs. Will, for example, was one of the local police surgeons and he earned substantial fees for being the medical officer for a couple of large, local factories.

Patsy and I were not complaining. I was earning extra money by writing books and articles and although I'd had to abandon my burgeoning career as a television doctor simply because I wouldn't hire a locum doctor and so could not leave the village to go to studios in London or elsewhere, we were managing very well. We grew much of our own food and in theory, we also had a small income from selling excess fruit and vegetables to Peter Marshall at the village shop. (In practice, there was sometimes a little difficulty in persuading Peter to part with the money he owed us.)

Miss Minchinhampton was one of the elderly patients whom I visited regularly at home.

Indeed, since I had taken over from Dr Brownlow I don't think she had ever visited the surgery at Bilbury Grange.

There was nothing really wrong with her apart from the fact that she was, in her own words, 'beginning to wear out a little'.

Her heart still did what it was paid to do. But it did so with increasing reluctance. And who can blame it or, indeed, complain?

How many machines can go through a complicated cycle of activity, 70 times a minute, for hour after hour, day after day, year after year, without a day off or a chance for a little light servicing?

Her lungs struggled to get enough oxygen into her blood.

Her arteries and veins were no longer examples of clean, efficient piping.

Her sight was no longer quite as sharp as it had probably once been and she had a pair of developing cataracts.

Her hearing was still working but if Peter Marshall had been offering her ears for sale even he would have had to mark them down as 'well used by previous owner'.

(Her hearing was not, however, quite as bad as she sometimes led folk to believe. I knew from personal experience that when she wanted to hear something she could do so with surprising clarity. She used an old-fashioned ear trumpet and first-time visitors were always required to subject themselves to the embarrassment of shouting into the business end of the device. I refused to use the ear trumpet.)

And her joints were, predictably, as well worn as might be expected after a good many years of use.

But Miss Minchinhampton did not take any medication and she didn't want any.

She moaned a little, she complained occasionally, she let it be known that she did not enjoy getting old and I think she took great pleasure from expressing her dissatisfaction with the world in general and her life in particular.

But she would not even consider taking medicines.

She regarded drugs as the work of the devil and saw no distinction between illegal drugs such as heroin and cocaine and the sort of medicaments that a doctor might prescribe.

Her state of good health was, in some ways, a minor miracle, for Miss Minchinhampton did everything she shouldn't do, and she had done everything she shouldn't have done for a very long time indeed.

She smoked cigars and she drank copious amounts of brandy and she had done so for so many years that her whole house smelt like a gentleman's club at midnight on a busy Saturday. The combination of cigar smoke and brandy fumes gave the house a unique smell of cedar wood which was, I have to confess, not entirely unpleasant and far preferable to some of the aromas present in homes occupied by elderly ladies and gentlemen.

The funny thing was that I had no idea just how old Miss Minchinhampton really was.

She talked occasionally about her parents and her grandparents and although it was clear from her conversation that her grandparents were no longer with us, I had never been quite clear about whether or not her parents were still in the land of the living. It seemed unlikely but one of the lessons you learn as a general practitioner is that few things are as impossible as they may appear to be. I once had a patient who was 81-years-old but who would not make a decision without asking his parents' permission. His father was 98-years-old and his mother was a year younger. In Bilbury, the elderly often still have their parents around and when they do, they always treat them with the utmost respect.

Miss Minchinhampton could have been in her 70s, her 80s or her 90s. I suspected that her true age was somewhere towards the top end of that range but she had smoked and drunk heavily all her life and these 'vices' can accelerate the ageing process.

As her physician I was, of course, the keeper of Miss Minchinhampton's medical records but these consisted of no more than an aged and very scruffy cardboard folder and a few equally scruffy pieces of cardboard on which Dr Brownlow and I had scribbled rather unhelpful remarks such as 'Surprisingly robust but complains that she feels she is wearing out', 'Not in bad condition for her age – whatever that is' and 'Much the same as last time'. This last comment had been written many times and had eventually become written as shorthand – MTSALT.

She had suffered a bout of tonsillitis just after the end of the Great War and in the 1920s she had sprained an ankle, though the records did not explain which ankle had been the unfortunate one, how it had been sprained or what treatment, if any, had been applied.

Under normal circumstances, a patient's medical records contain details of their date of birth, written in ink on the cardboard folder, but in Miss Minchinhampton's case, this portion of the folder had been torn off and had long ago disappeared.

I had always assumed that Miss Minchinhampton, who steadfastly refused to discuss her age with me, must have got hold of the folder and vandalised it herself. It didn't seem important. If she was so desperate to hide her age then what did it really matter?

'Would you like a cup of tea?' asked Miss Minchinhampton.

I said I would.

I have found, from experience, that Miss Minchinhampton is one of the patients I have who takes offence if I say 'no' to the routinely offered refreshments.

'I'll make you one,' said Miss Minchinhampton, with a sigh. 'I never drink tea at this time of day. I suppose you'll be wanting a biscuit too.'

She levered herself up out of her chair, moaning a good deal and muttering something to herself, and shuffled into the tiny kitchen at the back of her cottage. The kitchen was cramped and crammed with out-of-date equipment. There was a huge Belfast sink, a massive iron mangle, a wooden scrubbing board and an old-fashioned, black-leaded range. Everything in the kitchen looked as if it ought to have been in a museum. Or a scrapyard.

Her cottage had been built at some time in the early 19th century, and several attempts had been made to modernise it but none of the improvements had been done later than the early 1950s. There was an indoor lavatory and a sink with plumbing in the kitchen but there was no water upstairs and, indeed, there was no bathroom at all. There was an electricity supply, with sockets in the living room and the bedroom, but there was no central heating of any kind. The only heat came from an open fireplace in the solitary downstairs room. If hot water was required it had to be heated on the range.

Several minutes later Miss Minchinhampton returned, carrying a tray upon which she had placed a teapot, a cup and a saucer. The saucer was decorated with a teaspoon. There was also a milk jug and a sugar bowl. There were three digestive biscuits on a plate. One of them had a small portion missing.

She put the tray down on her dining table; a huge oak monstrosity which took up nearly a third of the room. I sat down on one of the four upright chairs positioned around the table. She sat down on one of the other chairs.

'It's my birthday soon,' said Miss Minchinhampton. She poured tea into the solitary cup and added a little milk. She then added two spoonfuls of sugar and stirred the resulting mixture.

I asked her the date.

'Two weeks today,' she replied.

'Do you want to tell me how old you'll be?'

'I certainly do not!'

'Are you going to have a party?' I asked her.

'I've never had a birthday party.'

'Never?' I asked, surprised. 'Not even when you were a girl?'

'Never,' said Miss Minchinhampton. She picked up the cup and tasted the tea. It seemed to pass the test. I didn't like to mention that she had made the tea for me. Indeed, to be honest, I was rather relieved. I'd seen inside her kitchen.

My older patients do sometimes forget things. It doesn't always mean that they're developing Alzheimer's disease, or any other form of dementia.

'My parents were very religious,' she said. 'They belonged to a rather strange sub-sect of the Quaker movement and they didn't believe in parties. Not even for children.'

'So there were no balloons, games or trifle in your house?'

'Certainly not,' replied Miss Minchinhampton. She sounded wistful and it wasn't difficult to tell that she was rather sad not to have had a childhood adorned with balloons and trifle. I felt rather sorry for her.

'Would you like to have a party?' I asked.

There was no reply so I repeated the question.

She sighed.

I repeated the question for a third time.

'I suppose so,' she said, feigning reluctance and disinterest.

'Maybe we could organise one.'

'If it would make other people happy.'

'I'm sure it would.'

'I don't leave my home,' she told me, with some certainty.

'I know that.'

'I haven't been out of this house since 1952.'

'Is it really that long?'

'It certainly is.' She paused and then looked me straight in the eye as though daring me to defy her. 'And when I do leave I will be travelling in a wooden box.'

I was accustomed to Miss Minchinhampton's unique mixture of determination and gloominess and so I simply smiled and nodded.

'Do they still make those coloured bits and bobs they put on the top of cakes?' she asked, unexpectedly/

'I think they do. I think they call them 'hundreds and thousands'. Some people call them 'sprinkles'. People also put them on the top of trifles.'

'I saw some once on a cake in a shop,' said Miss Minchinhampton wistfully. 'The cake was in the window. I thought the coloured bits and bobs looked very pretty.' She paused and didn't speak for a moment. I could tell that she was lost in a memory. There were tears in her eyes. 'My mother pulled me away from the window and said the cake was indecent and that the coloured bits were very frivolous and quite decadent.'

'They're certainly frivolous,' I agreed. 'But I don't think there's anything particularly decadent about putting coloured bits of sugar on top of a cake or a trifle for a party.'

Miss Minchinhampton pulled a handkerchief from her sleeve and dabbed at her eyes. 'I think I've got a fly in my eye,' she said. I noticed that she had dabbed both eyes.

'How old would you have been then?' I asked. 'Approximately?'

'I was seven,' replied Miss Minchinhampton, without hesitation. 'We were living in Wolverhampton. The shop with the cake in the window was a bakery and the man who ran it had a port wine stain on his right cheek. I know it is not right to say so but as a child I found him rather alarming. We never bought anything from the shop because we had a cook who made our bread. We weren't wealthy, just ordinary middle class, but people like us had cooks and maids in those days. My father was an assistant bank manager. It was quite a large branch. He used to wear a frock coat to work. He always looked very smart. I remember I had on a blue coat and a blue beret at the time. I used to have ribbons in my hair but I can't remember what colour they would have been. The ribbons would have been under the beret. My mother didn't approve of folderols but she allowed me the ribbons.'

We sat in silence for a while.

'Would you like me to ask Patsy to make you a trifle and put on some hundreds and thousands?' I asked her, quietly.

There was a long, long pause. 'Would it be possible to put them on the top of a cake?' asked Miss Minchinhampton. 'I think people might like that.' She closed her eyes. 'A sponge cake. With jam in the middle and white icing on the top.'

'And coloured sprinkles scattered on top of the icing?'

'Exactly. Quite a good number of them. And sprinkled right up to the edge of the cake. The jam was squeezing out of the side of the cake. It was definitely strawberry jam. I could see a strawberry.'

'Would you like candles on the cake?'

'No.' Miss Minchinhampton was quite definite. 'It didn't have candles.' There were tears forming again and she used the handkerchief to dab them away. This time she didn't mention the fly. 'I wouldn't want candles,' she said. 'There weren't any candles.'

'I'll see what we can do,' I promised her. 'But put it in your diary. Two weeks today. Miss Minchinhampton's birthday party.'

'I don't keep a diary,' said Miss Minchinhampton. 'Why would I keep a diary? No one ever comes to see me and I never go anywhere.' This was said with defiance, rather than self-pity. I had known her for some years and she had never seemed to be a woman to seek out or enjoy the company of others.

'Just a figure of speech,' I said softly. I stood up, put a hand on her shoulder for a moment and let myself out.

As I drove back to Bilbury Grange, I marvelled at the way we cling to some seemingly irrelevant memories and the impact tiny things can have on our lives. I suspect that Miss Minchinhampton had completely forgotten many of the things that had happened to her and which had, at the time of their occurrence, appeared to be life-changing. But she had remembered vividly the sponge cake which had strawberry jam squeezing out of the sides and the white icing covered with brightly coloured hundreds and thousands.

Planning the birthday party took Patsy and me much of the following fortnight.

We decided to invite just a small group of people with whom we knew that Miss Minchinhampton would be familiar: a few of her neighbours, Thumper Robinson and his lady, Anne, Patchy and Adrienne Fogg and my receptionist Miss Johnson. Thumper had done a good many odd jobs for Miss Minchinhampton and Patchy had purchased several pieces of china from her when she had been running low on funds.

We wrote out invitation cards and told everyone to bring balloons, birthday cards and small, wrapped gifts.

I decided that since Miss Minchinhampton was having a birthday party, her very first birthday party by her own account, then I would damned well make some effort to find out just how old she really was. I made a few telephone calls, hustled my way through a good deal of National Health Service red tape, and spoke to a variety of administrators in departments up and down the country. Since I was legally and morally responsible for Miss Minchinhampton's health and welfare, I had a good reason for desiring this simple piece of information. And eventually, I obtained the facts I needed.

Miss Minchinhampton was quite correct about the date in the calendar when her birthday should be celebrated but I was staggered to find out precisely how old she was – and which birthday she was due to celebrate.

When I checked the information I'd received, I talked things over with Patsy and she agreed with me that we should make a little bit of extra effort to commemorate the day.

Thanks to a friend on one of the national newspapers to which I contributed articles and columns, I got hold of a rather difficult-to-obtain telephone number in London. The very important gentleman to whom I spoke was, at first, reluctant to help. He explained that his office usually required several weeks' notice and it was only after a considerable amount of pleading that I succeeded in persuading him to bend the rules, make an exception and push through the arrangements I had requested.

Patsy herself had been responsible for preparing the jam filled sponge cake, icing it and covering it with hundreds and thousands. Peter Marshall had tried to sell her a packet of little silver balls as decoration but Patsy had insisted that she wanted coloured sprinkles and eventually Peter had found a couple of boxes of these. Patsy had managed to use up both boxes on the one cake – making sure that the hundreds and thousands were spread right to the edge of the icing. Patsy's mother, Mrs Kennett, had prepared a magnificent looking trifle (laced in honour of Miss Minchinhampton with generous helpings of brandy). And the two women had, between them, prepared a wide range of sandwiches, a collection of vol au vents and enough little sausages on sticks to feed a small army.

At last, the big day came.

Patsy and I drove to Miss Minchinhampton's cottage before the others. We were the advance party. We took a large supply of balloons, a boxful of silly hats and some paper plates, plastic glasses and plastic knives (all provided at a surprisingly reasonable price by Peter Marshall). Patsy had very sensibly decided that we would avoid a good deal of washing up if we used disposable plates and cutlery.

We also took a box of Miss Minchinhampton's favourite cigars, supplied by Peter Marshall, and two bottles of an excellent brandy which Frank Parsons of the Duck and Puddle had obtained for us at a very special price. These were the presents which Patsy and I had decided would be most gratefully received.

Miss Minchinhampton did not lock her front door and, like all those who visited her, I was in the habit of knocking and walking in without waiting for an invitation. Miss Minchinhampton said she preferred this because it saved her the effort of having to get up out of her chair.

When Patsy and I entered, carrying all the goodies, the old lady burst into tears.

They were not the easily disguised tears that I had seen before. These were not tears which could be passed off as 'I think I've got a fly in my eye'.

'Whatever is the matter?' asked Patsy, putting the tin in which we had brought the cake down on Miss Minchinhampton's dining table. She moved a chair and sat down beside the old lady.

Miss Minchinhampton did not reply but picked up an envelope, which was lying on the table in front of her and handed it to Patsy. It was a very smart blue envelope, well-made, much thicker and larger than the sort of envelope usually employed for sending letters or greetings, and the outside was marked with a message addressed to the Officer in Charge at the Delivery Office, commanding him in particular and the Royal Mail in general to deliver the item on the first available delivery on that very day. There was a note ordering the Officer in Charge to telephone Buckingham Palace to confirm that the letter was about to be delivered. Underneath this note there was a warning which would, I suspect, have curdled the blood of any Royal Mail employee: 'Failure to do so by 09.30 will initiate an enquiry from The Palace.'

I had never seen anything quite so impressive.

If an envelope could have come with a fanfare this one would have brought its own arch of trumpets.

'Open the envelope,' instructed Miss Minchinhampton.

We both knew what was inside the envelope, of course, and so it was no surprise to see a card, addressed to Miss Minchinhampton and congratulating her on reaching her 100th birthday. The card was signed 'Elizabeth R'. On the front of the card, there was a portrait of Her Majesty the Queen – wearing a tailored dress, three rows of pearls and a beautiful smile. The card even came with its own golden tassel.

It was well worth all the effort. Oh, it was well worth the effort.

'I didn't know it was my 100th,' said Miss Minchinhampton. 'I've never taken much notice of birthdays.'

'You really didn't know?' said Patsy.

Miss Minchinhampton shook her head. 'I knew it was close,' she said. 'But I've never kept track.' She pulled out her handkerchief and blew her nose. 'Did you arrange this?'

'The doctor did,' said Patsy.

Miss Minchinhampton looked at me. 'However did you know?'

'Aha!' I said, grinning at her. 'You'd be surprised what a doctor can find out if he puts his mind to it.'

'And it really is my 100th?'

'Really,' I said.

Just then the rest of the guests started to arrive. We waited until everyone was present, and Miss Minchinhampton's tiny cottage was filled with people, balloons and food. Everyone had brought presents.

Finally, Patsy took the cake out of the tin in which it had been transported.

Miss Minchinhampton burst into tears again. 'It's my cake!' she managed to blurt out before the tears started.

And it was, I have to admit, a dead ringer for the cake Miss Minchinhampton had described to me: the strawberry jam so thickly spread that it was oozing out of the side of the cake, the icing covered with a very generous quantity of hundreds and thousands.

Miss Minchinhampton lit one of her cigars. On her instructions, Patchy opened the brandy and served out generous portions, albeit in plastic glasses. Sandwiches were nibbled, trifle was much enjoyed and finally the cake was cut and slices were distributed.

'Happy Birthday' was sung with much gusto by the assembled choir.

We all stayed for a couple of hours, until it was clear that Miss Minchinhampton was tiring. I then had a quiet word with the other guests and they tactfully withdrew. Patsy collected together all the used plates, glasses and cutlery and put them into a rubbish bag. It took only a few minutes to clear away the debris.

'It was my first ever birthday party,' said Miss Minchinhampton. She was crying and smiling. I don't think I have ever seen more pure, unalloyed happiness than there was in her eyes. 'How did you know about the cake?' she asked me.

'You mentioned something about it,' I told her.

'Did I?'

I nodded.

'It was my cake,' said Miss Minchinhampton. She looked at the remains of the cake. There wasn't much left. 'Definitely my cake.'

'I hope it tasted as good as you'd imagined it would,' said Patsy.

'Oh, better,' said Miss Minchinhampton. There was the beginning of a new tear in one eye. 'Much better.'

'Not too decadent, was it?' I said.

She shook her head, looked up at me and smiled. 'No,' she said softly. 'It wasn't decadent at all.' She brushed the tear away with the back of her index finger. Another replaced it.

It was only seven o'clock in the evening but she was tired so we helped her up to bed. Patsy helped her undress and together we helped her into bed.

'I've had the best day of my life,' said Miss Minchinhampton quietly. She closed her eyes and nodded, as though agreeing with herself. 'I had to wait 100 years for it. But I want you both to know that it was the very best day of my life.' She held each of us by the hand, in turn, and smiled at us. I had known her for years but I had never seen her that way.

'I can die happy, now,' she said.

'But not yet,' I told her sternly.

She opened her eyes, looked at me and smiled. 'No, perhaps not quite yet,' she agreed.

Patsy and I stayed with her until she went to sleep.

And then we crept off downstairs, put the remains of the cake, complete with its hundreds and thousands, back into the old biscuit tin in which it had come, fastened the lid tightly and put the tin in Miss Minchinhampton's larder.

I picked up the rubbish bag which contained the debris from the party and Patsy and I went home.

It had been a good day in Bilbury.

A very good Bilbury day.

Cyril's Petard

Thumper Robinson, Patchy Fogg and I were sitting in the snug at the Duck and Puddle. It was one of those cold winter days that are a speciality of North Devon. Outside, a stern south-westerly wind was troubling the trees and doing nature's pruning; scattering dead branches and twigs far and wide.

Three workmen in yellow high visibility vests had, for reasons that were never entirely clear, dug a hole in the road and, having done this, they were now doing something that required flasks of tea and much standing around and chatting. They were warming their hands on their mugs of tea and probably deciding what to do with the hole.

An old man in a grubby mackintosh, who certainly wasn't local and whom I had never seen before, was standing nearby. He was watching them drink their tea and admiring the hole. I don't know where he had come from but I have noticed on many occasions that whenever workmen dig a hole there will always be a spectator or two available.

'I saw Cyril this morning,' said Thumper, sipping at his pint of Old Restoration; an unusually strong local brew which is reputed to have the alcoholic content more like that of a spirit than that of a beer. 'I tried to pretend I hadn't seen him but he collared me before I could get the truck started.'

Patchy and I immediately groaned in sympathy.

Cyril's full name is Cyril Rodney Arthur Player and he is our local pessimist. He has an unnatural ability to see the gloomy side of everything. And he delights in sharing his gloom. Frank, the landlord of the Duck and Puddle, went to school with him and reckons that Cyril never recovered from having parents who thought they were doing him a favour by giving him three Christian names but who did not realise that at the local school, it was common for pupils to be known by their initials. Going through your school years known to pupils and teachers as C.R.A.P. must have had an impact on a developing boy. I knew a boy called Samuel Andrew Dennis and to be S.A.D. was bad enough. To have been known as C.R.A.P. must have been torment.

'He asked me if I was worried that Mrs Kendall's cottage might attract squatters,' said Thumper.

'Is it still empty?' I asked. Mrs Kendall had died two months earlier. Her cottage was cold, dark and damp.

'I don't think even squatters would want to live in it,' said Thumper. 'There were rats living there for a while but they left. Probably too cold and dirty for them.'

'Why would squatters settle in Bilbury?' asked Patchy. 'Don't squatters want to live in places where there are clubs, bars, pubs and drug dealers?'

'It was just Cyril being Cyril,' said Thumper, dismissively.

Cyril is, without a doubt, the gloomiest person I know or have ever met. He is unremittingly pessimistic. He has an unerring capacity for finding the blackest cloud in any sky and a quiet determination to share the knowledge with the person most likely to be depressed by it. Mrs Kendall's former cottage stands no more than a quarter of a mile from the home which Thumper shares with Anne and their children.

Patchy, who was drinking a double Sheep Dip, sighed and shook his head. 'Someone should put Cyril on a spit and cook him over a slow fire,' he said, rather bitterly.

Patchy has never forgiven Cyril for asking him if he knew that the wall alongside his property was 'about to fail'.

Cyril claimed that he had noticed that the stone wall, which was something over six feet high, had a worrying looking bulge in its middle. 'Would you be able to live with yourself if it fell on a woman with a pram?' he had asked, before drawing a vivid word picture of the awful consequences.

Patchy, who had never noticed anything amiss with his wall, had been so worried by Cyril's foreboding that he had commissioned a surveyor to prepare a report on the wall's safety. The surveyor, who had confirmed that the wall was perfectly safe for another century or so, had presented Patchy with a bill for £60.

I should, at this point, perhaps remind readers that Sheep Dip is the name of a blended whisky made from 16 separate types of malt whisky. It is much favoured in Devon where farmers buy the stuff by the crate and then put it down in their accounts as an expense. They are helped in this slightly crooked endeavour by the fact that one of the large wholesalers, which specialises in selling animal feed, fertiliser and genuine sheep dip, also has this particular brand of whisky in stock. The result is that their customers can order twelve bags of sheep pellets, nine bags of fertiliser and two crates of Sheep Dip without anyone being any the wiser. As far as I know, the taxman has not yet worked out that the stuff the farmers are buying never gets close to a sheep's foot.

I don't think there is anyone in the village who doesn't suddenly discover an urgent appointment somewhere else if they see Cyril coming.

Mr Kennet, my father-in-law, was once asked by Cyril if he worried about his spring water drying up. Since the spring which supplied Mr Kennet's farm was also the main source of water for his livestock, this thought was a source of considerable distress for some weeks. In the end, Mr Kennet forked out several thousand pounds to have a dowser find a supplementary water source and for a drilling engineer to fit a water pump and an underground tank. What particularly upset him was the fact that he knew that the spring had never dried up in over a hundred years. And yet when Cyril had put the pessimistic thought into his head, it had kept him awake for a week.

Cyril had got under my skin on three occasions.

He once spent half an hour warning me about the stream which travels through our land. He pointed out that if the stream flooded it would almost certainly affect the cellars and ground floor at Bilbury Grange.

On another occasion, he took considerable delight in warning me that if the massive and wonderful copper beech which stands a few yards from our dining room window were ever to decide to prefer lying down to standing up then the trunk and upper branches would doubtless destroy that part of our house. That's the trouble with Cyril: his warnings always appear to be well-intentioned and based on logic.

The third occasion concerned the Rolls Royce which I had inherited from Dr Brownlow, my predecessor, and which was my mechanical pride and joy. 'Those old cars look very good,' he said, 'but you can't possibly think it's a suitable motor vehicle for a country general practitioner with a large rural practice. Old cars are far more likely to break down than modern ones and when they do break down, the chances are that the garage will have a hell of a job finding spare parts.'

As usual, the thing that really annoyed me was the fact that he was absolutely correct in everything he said. I didn't need anyone to say it.

Thinking about Cyril is always depressing so we ordered another round of drinks. Another pint of Old Restoration for Thumper, another double dose of Sheep Dip for Patchy and another small glass of 25-year-old Bunnahabhain for me. Bunnahabhain is a golden coloured malt whisky which I could ill afford to drink but could not afford to miss. Bunnahabhain is, I believe, the sweetest of all Scotch whiskies; smelling and tasting, as it does, of caramel, treacle toffee and Christmas. Patsy introduced it to me when she bought me a bottle one year as a Yuletide present.

'So how did you get rid of Cyril?' asked Patchy, when Frank had brought the drinks to our table and, after obtaining Gilly's permission, poured himself a small port. Gilly, who is Frank's wife, controls every aspect of the landlord's diet, for a little while ago he had a stroke which very nearly killed him. She has, without a doubt, saved his life and him from himself.

Thumper grinned. 'Got him hoisted high on his own petard!' he replied.

Patchy and I looked at him.

'I told him that you'd been to see a lawyer about that nonsense he said about your wall,' said Thumper. 'I said the lawyer told you that he thought you'd have a good case against him for wilful and deceitful misdirection.'

Patchy and I both frowned.

'What the devil is 'wilful and deceitful misdirection'?' I asked. I was still recovering from the fact that Thumper had known, and used, the word 'petard'.

'Buggered if I know,' replied Thumper with a shrug. 'I made it up; on the spur of the movement.' He grinned at us. 'It sounds good though doesn't it?'

We both agreed that it sounded very convincing.

'I told him the lawyer had said that you could sue him for damages and that unless you were in a very magnanimous mood he would probably be served with a summons any day now,' completed Thumper with a big smile.

'What did Cyril say?'

'He asked how much I thought you would be asking for.'

'What did you say?'

'I said I thought you would be demanding £5,000 plus costs.'

'£5,000!' exclaimed Patchy. 'Did he believe you?'

'He certainly did,' said Thumper. 'He went pale and scurried off home, muttering something about putting everything he owned into his wife's name.'

I suppose I should have felt sorry for Cyril, but I didn't. For years now, he has spread worry and stress and caused many people in the village to have sleepless nights. He has also caused many villagers to incur unnecessary expense. And I know of three very splendid and perfectly healthy trees which were taken down because the owners were worried that they might fall and crush their homes. Maybe Cyril would now be a little less anxious to cause unwarranted anxiety.

We all sipped at our drinks in silence for a while.

'You don't suppose there's anything in this 'wilful and deceitful misdirection' thing, do you?' Patchy asked me. 'I wouldn't expect £5,000, and I don't suppose Cyril has got that much anyway, but £1,000 would be fair, wouldn't it?'

I looked at him, to see if he was being serious. He was.

'Thumper made it up,' I reminded him quietly.

'Ah, yes,' said Patchy. He looked rather downcast. 'That would make a difference, I suppose.'

I ordered him another large Sheep Dip as consolation for the disappointment.

But Patchy is an antiques dealer. He never stays disappointed for long. He knows there is always the chance of another bargain discovery behind a worm-ridden wardrobe.

And since I couldn't order Patchy a drink without ordering one for Thumper, I asked Frank to bring another pint of Old Restoration.

'Another glass of Christmas for yourself, doc?' asked Frank who agrees with me that the Bunnahabhain smells of yuletide.

'Oh, I think so,' I said. 'It looks cold outside.'

'Do you think I ought to have another small port?' asked Frank.

I told him he had to ask Gilly.

He hurried away to consult the management.

While we waited for our drinks, I looked out of the window.

Outside it was still windy and the sky was overcast. The three men in high visibility jackets were still contemplating their hole. The man in the grubby mackintosh had been joined by two other spectators. I didn't recognise either of them. They weren't locals. I wondered where they had come from and how they had known there was a hole waiting for them to look into.

Life is full of mysteries.

But sometimes I think it's best to leave them for someone else to worry about.

On Their Holidays

Doctors who work in towns which deliberately make an effort to cater for holidaymakers and tourists have reported that their workload can double in the summer months.

During the winter, when the hotels and boarding houses are closed or nearly empty, doctors in a tourist area will find themselves living fairly leisurely lives. They have only to look after a relatively small population of locals. Hotels will be closed or near deserted and many owners of boarding houses will have closed their doors and their shutters and fled to Spain for a winter of rest and sunshine.

People who have holiday homes in the area will have gone back to their main homes, leaving their cottages, bungalows, chalets and caravans closed and shuttered for the winter. Seaside resorts can be empty, lonely and damp in the months from November to March.

But in the summer months, when the hotels are packed and the local caravan and camping sites have opened their gates, the very same doctors will work long days and nights providing medical services for patients whom they have never seen before, and whom the National Health Service officially describes as 'temporary residents'.

Most of the problems these patients bring with them are fairly easily treated. Sunburn, summer colds, cuts and bruises, insect stings, food poisoning and sexually transmitted infections are top of the list of ailments at any holiday resort.

In Britain, doctors who treat patients who are temporary residents can fill in a form and claim a fee for their work, and in areas of the country where holidaymakers are commoner than wasps at a picnic these sums can add up to a considerable part of the doctors' income.

Bilbury is close to some of England's most popular tourist areas, and it has many attractions of its own, of course.

But the village is not easy to find and apart from the village pub, the Duck and Puddle, there is no accommodation available for holidaymakers. No attempt is made to attract visitors to the village and Peter Marshall, who runs the village shop, admits that he sells no more than a few dozen postcards every year. He does a little bit of business selling soft drinks, biscuits and fruit to walkers, cyclists and motorists who have got lost, but he would never claim that selling to holiday makers makes a serious contribution to his bottom line.

Bilbury has had its moments, of course, and it has, without doubt or enthusiasm, toyed with tourism from time to time.

There was, for example, a period, now pushed to the backs of most minds, when the village was overrun with people responding to an article in which a writer had described Bilbury as Britain's healthiest village – and the 'perfect place to live'. For a while, the lanes had been clogged with visitors keen to see for themselves what made Bilbury so special.

And, more recently and perhaps most notably, there had been the ill-fated and never-to-be-repeated Festival which was held in a couple of fields and which drew huge crowds to Bilbury. I don't think it is an exaggeration to say that when the Festival's organiser decided that the event had been a commercial failure, and would not be repeated, there were celebrations in just about every house and cottage in the area.

But, on the whole, Bilbury is too far off the beaten track to see many strangers wandering through. We always welcome tourists who do come, for we are proud of Bilbury, but we don't promote ourselves in the way that some seaside resorts are prone to do.

As a result, it is a fact that some weeks I would see no tourists at all in my surgery.

But during the month of August, one year I saw four holidaymakers in as many days.

And the strange, and memorable, thing was that three of them had serious health problems. None of the three was simply a case of providing a simple treatment for a summer cold, blistered feet or a bout of hay fever.

Two of these case histories confirmed my theory that it is often so much easier for a doctor who has never seen a patient before to make a diagnosis than it is for a doctor who sees a patient regularly to make the same diagnosis.

The first patient, Mrs Danielle Studl, had come to the surgery complaining simply that she felt ill and inexplicably under the weather. She told me that she was in her early 30s but she looked ten years older. She was lined and seemed worn out. She wore a print summer frock that hung on her so loosely that it looked as if it were on a clothes hanger.

She had, she admitted, been poorly for some months but her symptoms had become worse since she'd arrived in North Devon a few days earlier. She and her family, one husband and three young children, had been staying in a caravan at a holiday park near to Combe Martin.

'Has the heat made things worse?' was my first question. The weather in Bilbury had been exceptionally warm for a week or more.

Mrs Studl admitted that it had. 'I can't stand this hot weather,' she told me. 'I feel bad about it but I keep hoping it will rain. The children are having a lovely time in the sunshine but it just seems to make me feel ill. I feel tired and weak and I'm constantly sweating.'

'Has your weight changed recently?' I asked her.

'It has,' she agreed. 'I've lost nearly a stone in the last six months.'

'Have you been trying to lose weight? Have you been dieting? On a slimming diet?'

'Oh no! I know you probably don't hear this often but I'd like to be a little heavier. My husband is always telling me I need to put on a bit of weight.' She subconsciously touched her chest.

'What's your appetite like?' I asked her.

Losing weight without trying is always a symptom that needs to be taken seriously. But some causes are more serious than others. And I was already beginning to feel that I knew what was wrong with Mrs Studl.

'I eat like a horse,' admitted Mrs Studl. 'I'm always hungry. And I eat more than my husband.'

'But despite this you're losing weight?'

She nodded.

'How do you sleep?'

'Badly! It takes me ages to get to sleep. And I wake up a lot. Do you think it's the sleeplessness that is making me tired?'

'It isn't helping,' I told her. 'Do you get palpitations?'

'Sometimes, I do, yes.'

'How are your bowels?'

'I have to go more often than used to be the case. I've had diarrhoea for a few days now. That comes and goes.' She leant forward in the chair and lowered her voice. 'Is it cancer, doctor? My neighbour's sister lost a lot of weight and she had bowel troubles. She had cancer. She was dead in six months.'

'No,' I told her firmly. 'I don't think you've got cancer.' I was now even more certain that I knew what was wrong with her.

'Hold out your hand, please,' I told her.

'Which one?'

'Either.'

She held out her right hand.

'Keep it as steady as you can.'

There was a clearly visible tremor in her fingers.

'I can't help it, doctor,' she said, almost apologetically. 'I just can't stop the trembling.'

I asked her to climb up onto my examination couch.

Two minutes later I was certain of the diagnosis.

Mrs Studl had very moist, warm skin and she had a fast pulse. Her heart was beating irregularly and she had a very wide pulse pressure – in other words, there was a massive difference between her systolic and diastolic blood pressure readings. I examined her neck but could find no abnormality.

'Are you sure it isn't cancer?' she asked, when she was sitting back in the chair on the other side of my desk.

'I'm pretty certain that you have a condition called thyrotoxicosis,' I told her. 'It's also known as hyperthyroidism. It isn't cancer.'

Mrs Studl looked puzzled. 'I thought people with that had swollen necks. My mother had a friend with thyroid trouble. She had a very swollen neck.'

'Sometimes patients have a goitre – a swelling in the neck,' I agreed. 'But not always.'

'And you think that's what is wrong with me?'

I nodded. 'I do. And the good news is that it can be treated.'

Mrs Studl started to cry.

I handed her the box of paper tissues which I always keep on my desk.

'I thought it was cancer,' she said quietly, when she'd wiped her eyes and blown her nose.

'No,' I said.

'What's the treatment? Do I need surgery? An operation?'

'Your doctor will need to give you some tablets,' I told her. 'He'll want to organise some tests and may send you along to the hospital to see a specialist. But the treatment will be medicine.'

I asked her how long she and her family were staying in Combe Martin.

'We go back on Saturday,' she said.

'Then there isn't much point in my organising tests here,' I told her. 'The results won't be back before you're on your way home. What is your doctor's name?'

She told me.

I picked up a piece of my notepaper and wrote a letter to her doctor. When I'd finished, I put the letter into an envelope and handed it to her.

'I've left the envelope unsealed for now,' I told her. 'So, you can read the letter and show it to your husband. Once you've both read what I've written put it back into the envelope and seal it. Then, as soon as you get back home, go and see your doctor and give him the letter.'

Mrs Studl took the letter, put it into her handbag and smiled. 'It's funny, isn't it? I feel much better than I did when I came in. And you haven't really done anything, have you?'

'It's thyrotoxicosis,' I told her again. 'Thyroid trouble. Not cancer.'

She smiled, nodded and left.

Thyrotoxicosis, caused by an overactive thyroid gland, is one of the easiest diagnoses for a doctor to make because the signs and symptoms tend to be so clear.

But, funnily enough, the opposite condition, one caused by an underactive thyroid gland, is also an easy diagnosis to make – especially if you have never seen the patient before and have not slowly got used to the patient's appearance.

Mrs Ethel Pelham came to the evening surgery the day after I'd seen Mrs Studl and I knew the minute she walked through the door, spoke to me and sat down exactly what was wrong with her. At least, I was pretty sure that I knew.

Mrs Pelham was in her early 60s. She moved slowly and was noticeably overweight. She had no expression on her face. It's a look you sometimes see with Parkinson's Disease but also with one other condition.

She did not, however, come to the surgery complaining of the problem I had so quickly diagnosed.

'I've got something in my eye,' she told me. 'It's been driving me mad but I couldn't see it to get it out and my husband is useless with medical things.'

It took me less than a minute to remove the very small fly from her eye. Her conjunctiva was red because she had rubbed it so much. I told her to blink a few times. While I extricated the fly, my hand touched her hair and that small contact confirmed my diagnosis.

'Oh, that's wonderful!' she said when I had taken out the fly. 'Such a relief.' Her voice was hoarse and her speech slow. She sounded like an old man who has smoked 60 a day for half a century.

'Another happy customer!' I said.

'Definitely, doctor.' She thanked me and started to get out of the chair.

'Before you go,' I said, 'do you mind if I ask you if you are being treated for anything by your doctor?'

She looked puzzled. 'No, doctor. I haven't seen my doctor for years.'

'Do you smoke?'

'Oh, no.'

'Have you been putting on weight in the last year or so?'

'I eat too much,' she said, defensively. 'Do you think I need to diet?' She seemed a trifle offended. I cursed myself for being so clumsy.

'I apologise,' I said. 'I asked you that for a reason. Do you get numbness and tingling in your hands or feet?'

'My hands, yes, I do. I get tingling in my hands.'

'Have you noticed that your skin is very dry?'

Now Mrs Pelham was looking puzzled. 'Yes, I have. How did you know that?'

'And have you noticed that your hair is very dry?'

'Yes. It's also getting thin and coarse.'

I nodded.

'You knew?'

I nodded. 'Do you suffer with constipation?'

'I do. You don't do magic tricks as well, do you? How did you know all this about me?'

'You dislike the cold weather more than ever?'

'Oh, I do. I can't stand the cold weather. Last winter my husband went mad because I had to have the heating on quite high all the time.' She looked at me and raised an eyebrow. 'You've spotted something, haven't you?'

'I think you have a bit of a problem with your thyroid gland,' I told her. 'It isn't working properly.'

'How on earth do you know that without doing any tests?'

'The things I've asked you about are classically signs and symptoms of an underactive thyroid gland,' I told her. 'The condition is called myxoedema or hypothyroidism and it can usually be treated fairly easily with some thyroid tablets.'

'You mean that if I take some tablets, my skin and hair will feel better?'

'Yes.'

'And that tingling, funny feeling in my wrists will go?'

'Yes.'

'And I won't need the heating so high in the winter?'

'Yes.'

'My husband is going to be very pleased.'

'Good.'

'And I'm going to be very, very pleased. When do I start taking these magic tablets?'

'When do you go home?'

'Tomorrow.'

'Then you need to go and see your own GP.' I reached for the notepaper again. 'I'll give you a letter to take to him. He'll want to do some tests. And then he'll prescribe some tablets.'

I wrote out the letter, put it into an unsealed envelope and handed it to Mrs Pelham. I told her she could read the letter and show it to her husband but that she should then seal the envelope and hand it to her doctor when she got back home.

'I'm glad that fly got into my eye,' she said, as she left.

The third call came two days and it was from a couple who were staying in a caravan site near Mortehoe.

I'm not sure why they called me because there were several doctors practising in the immediate locality. Maybe they just found my name in the local telephone directory and picked me out at random.

When I eventually found their caravan (not an easy task since there were several hundred identical caravans in a single very large field) I knocked on the door and found the couple were struggling to feed their baby.

They looked to be in their early 20s. Their name was Roberts.

He was called Peter. He was rather overweight and pasty looking and wore khaki, knee length shorts, a white T-shirt and one of those multi-pocketed gillets which are popular with photographers and fishermen. I couldn't see any cameras but there was a collection of fishing equipment stored in a corner of the caravan.

She was called Mary and she too was on the generous side of rather plump. She wore a pair of white shorts and a flowered bikini top which was rather overfaced. A large roll of fat hung over the front of her shorts.

The caravan, which seemed quite large, was crowded with the three of us and the baby inside. Part of the problem was the fact that every flat surface, including the seats, had things stored on them. There were piles of clothes everywhere. There were so many clothes on display that the caravan looked like the site of a jumble sale. I couldn't make my mind up whether taking a small baby away on a caravan holiday was brave or foolhardy, courageous or reckless.

'She keeps being sick,' said the young mother, who looked worried half to death. The baby was lying in a huge pram. The pram was so large that it took up much of the available space. I have no idea how they got it into the caravan. There were several used and greasy fish and chip wrappers around the place. Every last chip and piece of fish had gone. Even the little crunchy bits of batter had all been Hoovered up. All that remained were the fat stains on the paper, a couple of fish bones and a nauseating smell. There was also a rather unpleasant smell of baby vomit in the air. I looked around. All the windows were firmly shut.

'You need to give her some medicine to stop the sickness,' said the young father. He looked to me to be a rather aggressive, demanding sort of fellow.

'When did the vomiting start?' I asked.

'Two days after we got here,' replied the mother.

'And when did you get here?'

'Four days ago,' answered the father who sounded very fed up. 'The whole holiday has been pretty much ruined.'

'How old is the baby?'
'Six weeks,' said the mother.
'What's her name?' I asked.
'Tabitha.'
'That's a lovely name,' I said.
'I liked that television programme with the character called Tabitha.'

I must have looked rather blank.

'Bewitched.'
'Is that the name of the programme?'
'Didn't you ever see it?'
'I'm afraid not.' I was surprised that a couple had named their child after a character on a television programme. It wasn't something which I had come across before.

'Crumbs,' said the mother, pulling a disapproving face. I got the impression that my status and credibility had disappeared through the caravan floor.

'She needs some medicine to stop her being sick,' said the young father. He did not seem to me to be a man whom fatherhood became.

'Can I see her being fed?' I asked.
'She'll just be sick,' said the young father. 'It's a waste of milk.'
'I'll get the bottle,' said the young mother. She fetched a feeding bottle that was sitting in a saucepan of what I assumed was warm water and offered the teat of the bottle to the baby.

'You're not breastfeeding?' I said.
'Oh no,' said the young mother. 'Breastfeeding ruins a woman's figure.' The baby was now feeding with great enthusiasm. She looked well.

It seemed to me that fish and chips had already done a certain amount of damage to the woman's figure. Breastfeeding would not have caused any more damage.

'But breast milk is very good for babies, you know,' I said, not wanting to miss the opportunity for a little education.

'She's going to be sick now!' said the young husband. He sounded pleased in an 'I told you this would happen' sort of way.

And sure enough the baby was sick.

But this was no ordinary sickness.

The baby's vomit flew across the caravan with force, just missing me. The husband had craftily moved out of range.

'Ah,' I said, for now I was pretty sure that I knew what was wrong. 'Just undress the baby for me, please.'

The mother undressed the baby.

'And now feed her again.'

'She'll just be sick again,' moaned the husband. 'That'll mean more mess and more wasted milk. Can't you just give her something to stop the sickness?'

I ignored the husband and watched the baby's abdomen as she fed.

I could see a wave of peristalsis moving across the abdomen from left to right. I felt the baby's tummy and could feel a mass on the right side. It was the size of an olive. Now I definitely knew what was wrong.

'We're going to have to take Tabitha into the hospital,' I told the parents. 'She has a condition called pyloric stenosis. It is quite common and it can be cured.'

'What is it?' demanded the mother, who seemed genuinely concerned, though to say that she was worried might have been something of an exaggeration.

'Bang goes our holiday,' mumbled the father, with a sigh. He did not seem in the slightest bit concerned.

'The opening between the stomach and the bowel has become narrowed and so, as a result, food can't get through,' I explained. 'If she isn't treated, Tabitha will become dehydrated and not gain any weight. For some unknown reason, this condition usually affects boys but it can affect girls too.'

'How will they cure her?' asked the mother.

'A small operation,' I told her. 'It only takes about half an hour to do.'

'And then she'll be well again?'

'Yes.'

'Isn't there any medicine you can give her?' asked the father, who had clearly not been listening to anything I'd said.

'I'm afraid not,' I said. 'Do you have a car you could use to take Tabitha to the hospital?'

'Can't you ring for an ambulance?' asked the father. 'Aren't we entitled to an ambulance?'

'I could ring for an ambulance,' I said. 'Do you know where there's a telephone I could use?'

'There's one at the shop on the campsite,' said the young mother. 'A red phone box. But it doesn't work. It's been vandalised.'

'In that case I'll have to go back to my surgery and telephone from there,' I told them. 'Are you sure you don't want to take Tabitha to the hospital yourselves? I'll give you a letter to take with you and telephone them to let them know you're coming.'

'We're entitled to an ambulance,' said the young father.

'I'll send an ambulance,' I told them. 'Please look out for it so that you can meet them when they arrive. It took me nearly half an hour to find you.'

I then drove back to Bilbury Grange and telephoned the local hospital.

I never heard from the parents again but a couple of weeks later when I spoke to one of the paediatricians at the hospital. He told me that baby Tabitha had been treated quite successfully.

'I remember them,' said the paediatrician. 'The father was forever demanding things and going on about his rights. I thought he was a rather unpleasant fellow. I remember he wanted us to pay for his petrol when he came to the hospital to visit the baby.'

Finally, that week I saw a honeymoon couple who had come to North Devon on a camping holiday. Back in the 1970s, not every young couple went to the Maldives or the Caribbean on their honeymoon. Most were prepared to rough it, enjoy each other's company, and save a little extra money towards the deposit on a home.

These were the fourth (and fifth) patients I saw who weren't resident in the village. But, unlike the others, their problem was simple rather than serious.

They had spent a whole day sunbathing in the field where they'd camped. The new wife told me, with a delightful blush, that they had slept very little the previous night. The result was that they had both fallen asleep in the sunshine and they had, rather inevitably, ended up with unpleasant burns on their backs. Their skin was so tender that they couldn't bear to touch it or to have it touched.

They didn't need to go to hospital and they didn't need to have anything more complicated than some soothing lotion in the way of treatment.

But, sadly, I had to point out the obvious: that they would both have to lie on their fronts for a few days while their skin recovered.

'You mean you can't do anything to speed things up?' asked the new husband. 'You can't give us something to take away the soreness?' He sounded appalled and indignant at the same time.

'I'm afraid not,' I said, sympathetically but not very helpfully.

'But we're on our honeymoon!' complained the new wife who was clearly equally disappointed and, dare I say, frustrated by my inability to offer a speedier solution to their problem.

It would, I thought, be a honeymoon they would remember with rueful smiles and a little embarrassed laughter in future years.

But for the moment there were no smiles and definitely no laughter.

And not a lot of 'how's your father' or 'rumpy pumpy' either.

Shop Talk

'I think I might need a stitch in this, doctor,' said Archer Woodnutt, limping into the surgery.

He sat down, pulled up his right trouser leg and displayed a knee that was covered with a blood stained bandage.

'What on earth have you done to yourself?' I asked, when I'd unwound the bandage and revealed the damaged joint. There was a nasty looking, ragged cut in the skin over the upper end of his tibia, an inch or so below the bottom edge of his patella. I was relieved to see that the damaged area looked clean, and there were no signs of any infection.

'It's a bit embarrassing, to be honest,' said Mr Woodnutt. 'I was scrabbling around on the floor in the village shop when I caught my knee on a nail.'

I told him to climb up onto my examination couch. I then put on a pair of rubber gloves. Once he was comfortably settled on the couch I started to clean the wound, wiping away the dried blood. The two sides of the wound were a quarter of an inch apart and as I cleaned away the debris, the bleeding started again. There was clearly a need for a little sewing to be done. 'You'll need four or five stitches in that,' I told him.

'That many!' said Mr Woodnutt, clearly surprised. He looked down at his knee, examining it as though he were an expert in such matters. 'I thought one stitch would do it.'

'If I put in several stitches and keep them small and fairly tight then you shouldn't have too much of a scar,' I explained.

I filled a syringe with a local anaesthetic and injected a little around the wound. In my experience it is the biggest, strongest and youngest male adults who yelp the loudest if stitching is done without an anaesthetic.

'Oh, I'm not bothered about a scar,' said Mr Woodnutt. 'In fact, a nice scar is always a good talking point in bed.'

Mr Woodnutt is a 30 something bachelor with what Mrs Kennet, my mother-in-law, would describe an 'active social life'. He works as a freelance photographer, specialising in taking pictures of North Devon. His work regularly appears in most of the local Devon newspapers and magazines and occasionally in national publications. His photographs have also been used to illustrate the jackets of several books about the Devon countryside. Two of my books about my life in Bilbury have his photographs of the village adorning the dust jacket on the hard cover editions.

(Mr Woodnutt was not a little put out when it was drawn to his attention that a photograph on the cover of one of the earliest books had been taken by my good friend Thumper Robinson. Thumper takes what he usually calls 'snaps' and uses a camera which probably costs considerably less than the bag which Mr Woodnutt uses to carry his collection of expensive and impressive equipment. It was, I suspect, for this reason that we had never become friends. I arranged for Thumper's photograph to be used simply because I liked it.)

An endlessly optimistic man, Mr Woodnutt used to play football for the village football team.

(This was not a particularly praiseworthy achievement since the village usually had difficulty in finding eleven men under the age of 90 who could be described as 'fit' and who were prepared to wear shorts and run around in a muddy field for 90 minutes.)

I remember the occasion when, to his and everyone else's surprise, Mr Woodnutt scored a goal. It was his first goal in a dozen matches and only the second time the team had scored a goal in the whole season.

During the celebrations in the Duck and Puddle that evening, Mr Woodnutt, who had spent several hours describing his achievement in ever-growing detail, was overheard telling a comely companion that he had only needed two more goals for a hat trick.

'I never know what to talk about after doing it,' said Mr Woodnutt, whose life seemed to revolve around his adventures in the bedroom. 'I reckon that even a scruffy little scar should be worth five or ten minutes of idle chit-chat. How did you get that? Did it hurt? Were you very brave? That sort of thing. I'll have to work up a nice little story about being injured while taking pictures in a war zone somewhere.'

'There'll be a scar,' I promised him. 'But it will be as neat as I can make it.'

When stitches are placed very close to one another, there is a better chance of the two edges of a wound coming together smoothly and considerably less chance of a large scar developing.

'You didn't have to bother with any anaesthetic,' said Mr Woodnutt, who had carefully, and probably wisely, waited until I had finished giving the injections before announcing that he didn't need them.

'What on earth were you doing scrabbling around on Peter Marshall's floor?' I asked as I threaded a needle with a length of black silk.

'Peter has reorganised his shop and put all the cheapest products on the bottom shelves,' explained Mr Woodnutt. He shrugged. 'The stuff on the eye level shelves is much the same but it costs more.'

'Oh dear,' I sighed. It seemed that this was yet another building block in the legend that is Bilbury's solitary retailer; another contribution to the Peter Marshall story.

It has been said that the average shopper knows the prices of only a very small number of grocery items – milk, bread and eggs for example.

This may be true in big towns and cities but it isn't true of Bilbury. Most of the village's inhabitants don't have much money and they tend to be careful and more knowledgeable. There is a constant battle between Peter, on the one side, who is forever trying to keep his prices high to maximise his profits, and the rest of the villagers, who are forever looking for lower priced items so as to reduce their bills.

Everyone, including Peter, knows that if the prices in the local shop rise too high then villagers will decide that it is worthwhile making the long and expensive trip into Barnstaple to do their shopping.

However, I confess that I never fail to be surprised by Peter Marshall's skills at finding new ways to part his customers from their money without actually losing their custom to the supermarkets in Barnstaple.

For as long as I can remember he has kept all the necessities, items such as bread and milk, right at the back of his shop so that customers who want basic comestibles must walk through the entire shop and resist the temptation to purchase a can of quail's eggs, a new mousetrap or a brand new hand crafted rolling pin.

There are some in the village who believe that Peter acquired his ideas about retailing by studying the successful American supermarkets but there are also some who believe, rather whimsically it has to be admitted, that Peter is the originator and that other retailers around the world have copied his ideas for maximising profits.

Since I once saw Peter studying a copy of an American magazine produced for retailers I am, sadly, a realist in this matter and a believer in the former viewpoint.

'Do you remember that time when Peter read that shops which played music sold more stuff?' I asked Mr Woodnutt.

Mr Woodnutt laughed heartily. 'He only had a wind up gramophone and a recording of that chap who had a hit with the Laughing Policeman,' he remembered. 'Peter spent all his time winding up the gramophone and his customers got so fed up with the laughing policeman that they got out of there as fast as they could – often without bothering to buy the thing they'd gone in for in the first place.'

I put in the first stitch and Mr Woodnutt winced.

'Did that hurt?'

'No, not really hurt,' he admitted. 'But I felt it going in.'

I looked at him.

'Well, just about felt it,' he said. 'It didn't hurt though.' He looked a trifle pale.

'Do you feel faint?' I asked him.

'Just a bit queasy,' he said.

'Then don't look.'

He looked in the direction of the window. The wisteria which grows up around my consulting room window was in full bloom and the lilac flowers looked magnificent. My small lemon tree, which stands on the windowsill had its first fruit and the lemon was nearly ripe. There were also a couple of new flowers visible. They smelt wonderful. It was my first lemon. I had been watching it develop for weeks.

'Is this really a lemon tree?'

'It is.'

'Marvellous. I've never seen one before. Does it produce much fruit?'

'That's its first lemon. It's taken two years to get to this stage and Patsy reckons that one lemon has cost me a fiver in special plant food.'

'Crumbs!' said Mr Woodnutt. 'It smells wonderful doesn't it?'

It was true. The small lemon tree gave the consulting room a wonderful fresh smell, especially when there were flowers on it.

'Do you remember that time when Peter Marshall had a theory that if his shop smelt good then people would feel good and buy more stuff?' asked Mr Woodnutt.

'That idea he definitely picked up from one of those trade magazines he reads!' I agreed. 'But instead of making sure his shop smelt of ground coffee or baking bread he opened a huge bag of a particularly toxic smelling brand of fertiliser and left it just inside the doorway.'

'He'd bought two tons of garden fertiliser,' remembered Mr Woodnutt. 'But the stuff wasn't selling very well because everyone around here knows a farmer with a horse or two and so good manure isn't actually in short supply. Peter thought that if people smelt the stuff they'd want to buy it.'

'But for three days hardly anyone went into the shop to buy anything!'

'Mrs Todmorten stood outside in the rain, refused to enter the shop and handed Peter a list of what she wanted. She made him bring it all out to her and she wouldn't even go into the shop to pay her bill. She said the shop smelt worse than the public lavatory at the bus station in Barnstaple.'

'Do you remember that time he decided to charge shoppers sixpence in old, proper money to enter the shop. It must have been in around 1965 – well before the currency was decimalised. He said he'd had tourists go into the shop and just look around and that they were wearing out his floor boards without spending any money.'

'Am I right in thinking that the sixpence was refunded if a purchase was made?' asked Mr Woodnutt.

'Absolutely!' I agreed. I tied off the third stitch in a rather neat knot. Mr Woodnutt seemed pleasantly distracted and was no longer even wincing when the needle entered the skin on one side of the gash and left it on the other side.

'I seem to remember that your mother-in-law organised a boycott of the shop in protest,' said Mr Woodnutt.

'She certainly did! We were very proud of her. Peter Marshall stuck his heels in and for a day and a half I don't think he sold anything. Then he relented and withdrew the sixpence charge claiming that it had only been an experiment.'

'And then there was the Christmas when he organised a Lucky Dip,' said Mr Woodnutt. 'Peter filled an old barrel with sawdust, wrapped some holly around the edge of the barrel and buried prizes in the sawdust.'

'I remember that!' I said. 'He charged 50 pence a go but all the prizes were worth far less than 50 pence. I remember pulling a very small can of beans out of the sawdust and being very disappointed. Peter said that he had to charge 50 pence to cover the cost of the sawdust and the barrel and that we should be grateful because we were paying for the experience and the excitement.'

'Then there was the time when he started selling foods in pairs. I remember you could buy a jar of coffee and a bottle of pickled gherkins together.'

'But the price for the two items was never any cheaper than it would have been if you'd bought them separately,' I said. 'Sometimes he rounded up the price and so if you bought his 'special offer' you ended up paying more than if you'd bought the things separately.'

Just thinking of Peter's little tricks always made me smile. Everyone in the village was wise to his money-making scams. And I very much doubt if many tourists were taken in by them.

'I remember pointing out to Peter that there was never any logic to the pairing of items he was selling together. One week he had what he called a 'very special triple offer'. If you bought a packet of custard, a packet of envelopes and a jar of lemon curd you could get the lot for exactly the same price that you'd pay if you'd bought them all separately. I couldn't help wondering how many people went into his shop looking for a packet of custard, a packet of envelopes and a jar of lemon curd. I asked him why he didn't sell tea and milk together as one of his special offers and he replied that if people bought a packet of tea they would probably buy a bottle of milk anyway.'

I knotted the last stitch, put some antibiotic cream onto the wound to prevent any infection developing and then sat back to admire my handiwork. Even if I say so myself, it wasn't a bad bit of suturing. I'd managed to squeeze in six stitches.

'You'll need to come back in a week or ten days,' I told my patient. 'I'll check that it's healing properly and if it is I'll take out the stitches. But come back sooner if the area around the wound goes red or you develop a temperature.'

'Don't the stitches just dissolve and disappear?' asked Mr Woodnutt. 'I read somewhere that they make stitches that just get absorbed into the body.'

'Those suture materials are great for internal suturing, but these stitches are made of silk and have to be removed,' I told him. 'The suture materials that are absorbed can cause more scarring because they tend to cause local inflammation.'

'Silk, eh?' said Mr Woodnutt, impressed. He looked down at his knee for the first time since I'd finished. 'Not bad! You've made a neat job of that, doctor.' He jumped down off the couch and pulled down his trouser leg.

'Careful!' I told him. 'No football, no cycling and nothing too strenuous. I don't want you tearing my nice, neat stitches.'

Mr Woodnutt, repaired and ready again for the world, thanked me again, waved a cheery goodbye and tottered off.

I couldn't help noticing that he was now affecting an even more pronounced, and definitely unnecessary, limp than the one he'd had when he'd arrived in the surgery, and I suspected that by the time he reached the Duck and Puddle that evening his tangle with a nail in a dark corner of Peter Marshall's shop would have become a considerably more substantial confrontation; a dive to escape from a moving car or an encounter with a dangerous dog while attempting to snatch a photograph of some celebrity visiting the bright lights of Ilfracombe.

My next patient, Miss Harriett Wilson was blushing bright red when she entered and I suspected that Archer Woodnutt, who is known in the village and the surrounding area to be an outrageous flirt, had probably said something to her as they had passed; him on the way out and her on the way in to my consulting room. I noticed that she was walking very gingerly as though the very act of putting one leg in front of the other was painful.

I said 'good morning', pointed to the now vacant chair and invited her to sit down.

'I think I'd better stay standing if you don't mind, doctor,' said Miss Wilson. She bent her knees slightly and put her shopping bag, an ancient raffia thing down on the floor. The shopping bag seemed quite full of groceries. Though she had put down her shopping basket, Miss Wilson kept hold of her handbag. 'I'm a little worried that if I sit down I might not be able to get up again.'

Miss Wilson is a skinny little thing in her late forties; she is as pale as a country snow bank, though I know for a fact that she is not anaemic. She always reminds me of a sparrow and she can't weigh much more than a small bird. Certainly, two of her would have not weighed as much as the average, modestly sized adult.

She used to be a shorthand-typist working for the Inland Revenue but she resigned from her post when her grandfather died and left her a tiny, thatched cottage on the outskirts of Bilbury. She now lives on the income she receives from her savings and the little money which her grandfather left her along with the cottage. It is, I suspect, a rather meagre income which doesn't leave much room for treats and extravagances.

She once described herself to me as 'a bit of a virgin'. At the time, I had not found the courage to ask her for a definition of 'a bit of a virgin' and it still seemed to me to be a rather improbable, not to say impossible, concept. Still, I am sure she knew what she meant by it.

I could hardly believe my ears when she told me that she had done something to her back while scrabbling around on the floor at the back of Peter Marshall's shop.

'He's put all the lower priced items at floor level, hasn't he?' I said with a sigh.

Miss Wilson seemed surprised that I knew about Peter's latest trick. 'His prices are always a little on the high side,' said Miss Wilson, when she had confirmed the information I'd been given by Archer Woodnutt. 'But the bus fare to Barnstaple is quite expensive and the buses aren't very regular. So it's no more expensive to shop at Mr Marshall's.' She moved from one foot to the other. 'My mother, God rest her soul, taught me the value of money.' She paused, stretched, rubbed her back and fiddled with her watch for a moment. 'It's just as well,' she continued, 'for I have to watch my pennies.' I knew that this admission wasn't easy for her to make. She is a proud woman, always immaculately turned out. Today she was wearing a flowered summer dress, a light blue cardigan with pockets and a straw hat with a yellow ribbon around the brim and two red cherries attached to the ribbon. There was a ladder in the knee of one of her stockings, almost certainly a result of her having had to kneel on Peter Marshall's rough, wooden floorboards.

I hoped that her scrabbling around on the floor had saved her some money and I decided that when I had finished my morning surgery, I would drive to Peter's shop and have a stern word with him. I'd had an idea which would, I rather thought, prove effective at forcing him to abandon his latest profit boosting wheeze.

I know that running a village shop isn't an easy way to make a living (around the country many have closed and there are now thousands of English villages and hamlets which have no village shop at all) but I happen to know that Peter does better than most shopkeepers and from to time he needs to be reined in a little.

It didn't take long to discover that Miss Wilson hadn't done anything serious to her back. 'Go home, take two soluble aspirin tablets every four hours, rest and put a hot water bottle against the part of your back where the pain is at its worst.'

'What have I done?' she asked. 'Is it a slipped disk?'

'No, no, it's not a disk. You've just strained muscles in your back. They'll feel sore for a day or two but you'll soon feel fine.'

'The best value tinned pears were in a very difficult position,' said Miss Wilson. 'I had to stretch to reach a tin.'

'I'll have a word with Peter,' I promised her. I went into my small dispensary, filled a bottle with soluble aspirin tablets and took them out to her. I repeated the instructions I'd given her. 'How are you going to get home?' I asked her.

'I'll have to walk, doctor,' said Miss Wilson.

I looked at the single medical records envelope on my desk.

'No, you won't,' I told her. 'Go back into the waiting room, make yourself as comfortable as possible, and when I've finished the surgery I'll take you home. I've only got one more patient to see.'

'Oh I couldn't put you to that much trouble!' protested Miss Wilson.

'Miss Wilson!' I said sternly. I gave her my sternest look. It always makes Patsy laugh but some people find it slightly intimidating. 'If I find that you've gone when I come out of the surgery I'll be very cross.'

'I'll wait, doctor!' said Miss Wilson timidly.

My final patient of the morning was a woman called Hilda Musbury.

Mrs Musbury is a lonely widow who likes to talk.

She is built in the shape of a duck and, through her own brand of queue management, always manages to arrange things so that she is the last patient I see. She is convinced that I enjoy our conversations just as much as she does and she arranges to be the last patient, so she frequently tells me, so that we can both enjoy a good, long chat without being interrupted.

The truth is that I find our little chats about as much fun as root canal surgery but I feel rather sorry for her and usually talk, or more accurately, listen to her for a while. However, on this occasion I really didn't have the time for a chat about the weather and her garden. I have long believed that doctors should listen, rather than just talk, to their patients but sometimes there have to be limits. And this was one of those occasions when I really didn't have time to sit and listen to Mrs Musbury's commentary on the state of her lawn, the vicissitudes endured by her brother in New Zealand (it wasn't difficult to understand what had driven him to emigrate to the other side of the world) and the plots of her favourite television soap operas.

I couldn't sit around because I had promised to take Miss Wilson home, I had several home visits to do and I wanted to call in on Peter Marshall.

'It's lovely to see you, doctor!' said Mrs Musbury, breezing into the surgery as though we were old friends. She wandered over to the windowsill and examined my lemon tree. 'Your lemon is ripe!' she said. And before I could stop her, she had plucked the lemon from the tree. She held it up, as though it were a prize. 'You don't mind do you, doctor?' she said. 'I expect you've had hundreds of lemons from it already. I'd love to take this one home. I love a slice of lemon in my Earl Grey tea.'

I was horrified and very cross.

It was my first ever lemon.

I'd been watching it grow for an inordinate length of time. But what could I say that wouldn't sound mean or churlish? Besides, it was now too late for the lemon had been plucked.

I had been looking forward to making a sort of ceremony out of plucking the lemon. I'd thought that Patsy and I could say a few words, praise the lemon tree and then twist and pluck the lemon jointly.

I muttered something that probably sounded like approval, though to be honest I would have happily throttled Mrs Musbury if I had thought it likely that I'd have been able to get away with it. I sometimes think that the parameters for justifiable homicide ought to be expanded and on this occasion, I definitely felt that the crime of unauthorised lemon plucking ought to be on the allowable list.

'I do enjoy our little chats,' said Mrs Musbury. 'But I sometimes think I need more of a challenge in my life. Something to get my teeth into. Maybe I should learn a language? What do you think? Hindi, perhaps? Or take up the banjo? Or do some mountaineering? Something like that. I could go to the Himalayas. Or join an orchestra of some kind. They call them bands these days don't they?'

I didn't reply. I was struggling to get my head round the idea that there might be some connection between Hindi, banjo plucking and climbing snow clad mountains.

'I bet your Patsy wonders what we get up to in here, chatting away about things,' said Mrs Musbury, settling into the patient's chair and making herself comfortable. She sniffed my lemon and then dropped it into the dark and impenetrable recesses of the massive black leather handbag she took with her everywhere she went.

'I'm afraid I can't stop and chat,' I told her, rather brusquely. 'I've got some urgent things to do this morning.'

'Oh!' said Mrs Musbury, clearly rather annoyed. 'Oh, well, never mind. You go off and do whatever it is that needs doing. I expect you'll be doing something with that Miss Wilson. Taking her home, perhaps? She was in the waiting room looking rather under the weather and just a little sorry for herself. I'll just make myself comfortable here and wait until you get back.'

Mrs Musbury can be a little poisonous occasionally; especially when she feels put out.

'No good I'm afraid,' I said firmly. 'I have no idea when I'll be back.'

I stood up, helped her out of the chair and ushered her towards the door.

'I need a bottle of my special tonic,' she said quickly. 'That tonic you make up just for me.'

The tonic for which she has such affection is not as special as she imagines. It's a mixture which I make up and prescribe for quite a number of neurasthenic patients. It is dark green in appearance, it smells rather toxic and it has a bite that promises effectiveness. I hurried into the dispensary, found a bottle of the stuff and hurried back out with it clutched in my hand.

'Here you are!' I said. 'I thought you'd probably be in today and so I made this up for you earlier.' I hoped that my nose wouldn't grow too long.

Mrs Musbury put the tonic into her bag, alongside my lemon, and after telling me that she'd back for a chat that evening, departed in rather a bad mood.

I read, checked and signed a couple of urgent letters which Miss Johnson had left on my desk and picked up the details of the home visits which had been requested by telephone while I'd been doing the morning surgery. I then gathered the medicines I knew I'd need for the patients I had to see, popped into the kitchen to say goodbye to Patsy who was busy making vegetable pasties and then collected Miss Wilson from the waiting room.

'I've never been in a Rolls Royce before,' said Miss Wilson, climbing rather cautiously into the front passenger seat.

'It is a very old one,' I pointed out.

'Oh yes, but it's beautiful!' said Miss Wilson. She winced as she tried to get herself comfortable. 'It used to belong to Dr Brownlow, didn't it? I remember seeing him driving it when I visited my grandfather as a girl.' She gently ran her fingers over the beautifully matched walnut fascia.

'She's been the official practice car for the best part of half a century!' I said proudly. 'And apart from the old banger I drove when I first came to Bilbury the only official practice car. Before he bought this car, Dr Brownlow used to do his calls by horsepower.'

'Really? He rode a horse?'

'Sometimes. Especially at night and for emergencies. But he also had a trap which he would ride in when doing his routine daily visits.'

We had reached Miss Wilson's cottage. I stopped the Rolls, parked it on a small stretch of neatly trimmed verge and climbed out so that I could help Miss Wilson out of the car and into her cottage.

'Take the aspirin, fill a hot water bottle and move about as much as you can,' I told her when we were inside. 'But move gently.'

'You don't think I should go to bed?'

'Oh, no! You'll stiffen up if you do. Don't sit in one position for too long. And keep moving and bending your back as much as you can without doing anything painful. Nothing has been damaged. Ring me if it doesn't gradually improve.'

I left Miss Wilson in her kitchen boiling a kettle so that she could fill a hot water bottle and make herself a cup of tea. I have great faith in both these remedies. A hot water bottle is the best way of applying heat directly to an area of muscle which is sore. And a cup of tea is, of course, the traditional English way of responding to any sort of crisis.

Neither of the two visits I had to do was particularly urgent.

One request was to visit Enid and Harry Burrows who required fresh supplies of their medications. The other was from Olive Robinson, Thumper's much loved aunt, who simply wanted another bottle of the pills she takes to control her slightly raised blood pressure.

Since the practice had started dispensing medicines, my workload had increased considerably but there was no doubt that as far as the patients were concerned it was a much more convenient way of doing things.

In the old days, I would hand out a prescription and the patient would have to arrange to obtain the prescribed medication from a pharmacy in Barnstaple. Now that I had managed to persuade the authorities to allow me to dispense my own medicines, I could simply hand over the required medicines and the patient could start their treatment straight away. Once a day a van would come from a pharmaceutical wholesaler in Exeter and would bring fresh supplies of basic drugs together with supplies of anything unusual which we need. Patsy had taken on the responsibility of maintaining the records of the drugs we had in stock. She kept two large notebooks.

In one she had a list of all the standard medicines, the antibiotics, contraceptive pills, painkillers and heart medication, and in the other she listed unusual or special requirements. I also kept a third, smaller notebook in which I kept a record of the drugs such as morphine which were controlled under the Dangerous Drugs Act. I had to make a note every time I used a drug of this type, detailing the date, the name of the patient, the drug and the quantity prescribed.

When I'd finished the calls, I drove around to Peter Marshall's shop where I found the proprietor sorting through a huge pile of old crossword puzzle books. He was putting some of the books onto one pile and some onto a second pile.

'What on earth are you doing?' I asked him.

He explained that he had bought a huge pile of old crossword puzzle books from a charity shop in Barnstaple. All the books had been filled in, the crosswords completed, and the charity had wanted to get rid of them since they had no perceivable resale value.

'That doesn't answer the question,' I pointed out. 'What are you doing with them?'

'I'm sorting them into two piles,' he explained. 'The ones on this pile have all been completed in ink and they're no good at all. They'll have to be sold as scrap paper. But the ones on that pile have been completed in pencil and if I rub out all the pencil entries I'll be able to resell the books as new.'

I stared at him. 'But it'll take you hours!'

'What else is there to do in the evenings?' asked Peter. 'If I go to the Duck and Puddle it will cost me money. If I stay here and rub out crossword book entries I'll be making money.'

I just looked at him in astonishment.

'I can rub out all the entries in a puzzle book in just under half an hour,' he told me. 'So if I start at seven and go on until midnight, I can clean ten books in an evening and then put them on sale in the shop the next morning.' He looked at me quizzically. 'I don't suppose you and Patsy would like to earn a little extra in the evenings?'

'No thank you.'

'I'll provide the rubbers. I've got some new soft erasers that don't tear the paper.'

'No thank you.'

'Suit yourself. Let me know if you change your mind.'

I told him that I didn't think it very likely.

'You don't know of a decent ink solvent, do you?'

'Ink solvent?'

'For the crossword books which have been filled in with ink.'

'No, Peter. I don't know of an ink solvent you could use.'

'I tried some bleach but unless you dab out each letter very carefully, you remove the printed lines of the crossword. And if you put on too much bleach, the stuff burns a hole in the paper. I tried that white stuff typists use to cover up their mistakes but the people who print these crossword books use very cheap paper which is grey and the white blobs stand out and I think people might know that the books weren't new. Some of these publishers... '

'I saw two patients this morning who'd been injured while crawling around at the back of your shop looking for the low priced items you've hidden down at ground level,' I said, interrupting what threatened to be a tirade against publishers who used cheap grey paper for cheap paperback crossword books.

Peter stared at me and frowned. 'Who?'

'Can't tell you,' I told him. 'Medical confidentiality. But one of them has a badly cut knee.'

'Oh that was that Woodnutt fellow. He wanted me to pay for the rip in his trousers. I sent him packing. I can't be expected to make sure all the nails in my floorboards are hammered down nice and smoothly just so that people like him don't snag their trousers.'

'Peter, I really came to see you as a friend,' I said softly, leaning towards him as though I didn't want anyone to overhear. There wasn't anyone in the shop but Peter leant towards me, as though eager to share confidential information. 'You're going to get sued,' I told him.

'Sued!' said Peter, looking startled and leaping back a couple of feet. 'Why would he sue me? It was just a little tear. They weren't new trousers And a bit of blood. Nothing much.'

'No, no, I don't mean that he is going to sue you,' I said. 'Not yet.'

'Not yet?'

'But someone will sue you.'

'They will? Who will? I'll ban them from the shop.'

'If you keep the lower priced stuff on the floor at the back of the shop where people have to crawl around in the dark then someone is bound to sue you. Not a villager, perhaps. But a stranger. A visitor. Maybe a rich German just passing through.'

'You think so?'

'I'm sure so,' I said, nodding.

'What do you think I should do?'

'Bring all the cheaper brands back to the front of the shop where people can find them easily without having to scrabble around on the floor.'

There was a long pause, during which Peter examined my face carefully. He was, I knew, trying to tell if I was pulling some sort of fast one. 'You think someone might sue me?' he asked at last.

'I'm certain they will,' I assured him. 'As sure as eggs are eggs.'

'As sure as eggs are eggs?'

'Definitely.'

'Hmm. I'd better move the stuff round again.' He thought for a moment. 'I'll put the tinned rice pudding down on the floor at the back of the shop. No one ever buys that stuff anyway.'

'Good idea!' I said. And to show that there were no hard feelings, I bought one of the resuscitated and rejuvenated crossword books from which he had erased all the answers.

'See!' said Peter, proudly. 'I told you there'd be a market for them. You were about to scoff weren't you?'

'Not in a million years,' I said.

It occurred to me that at the rate I was going, my nose would be three feet long before I got back to Bilbury Grange. I slipped the crossword book into my pocket. It would, I knew, amuse Patsy when I told her the story of Peter's latest wheeze.

'Oh, before you go,' said Peter suddenly, as I strode towards the Rolls.

I turned back.

'I'm opening an estate agency,' announced Peter.

'Splendid!' I said. 'The village could do with one. But I'm afraid Bilbury Grange isn't for sale.'

'No, no, no,' said Peter impatiently. 'I didn't think for a minute that it was. But I'm looking for an estate agent to handle the agency for me. I need someone who is easy going and bubbly bordering on talkative; someone with time on their hands and prepared to work on commission. I'd do it myself but I'm too busy looking after the shop.

I want someone who can move around the village, putting up signs, showing houses to prospective buyers, that sort of thing.'

'Not my line,' I said firmly.

'Don't be so damned obtuse!' said Peter crossly. He is renowned for having had a humour extraction some years ago. 'You know just about everyone in the village. I just wondered if you might know someone suitable.'

I thought for a moment and then shook my head. 'No one springs to mind.'

'I need someone who's a bit pushy and who won't take no for an answer,' continued Peter, warming to his theme, 'someone who can persuade both the seller and the buyer that they're on their side.'

I shook my head.

'Well let me know if you think of anyone suitable.'

I headed for the car when suddenly it came to me: the perfect solution – the answer to Peter's problem! Who could possibly fit the bill more snugly than the patient who only that very morning had told me that she wanted a challenge in her life? I turned back.

'Mrs Musbury!' I cried.

'Mrs Musbury?'

'You must know her!' I said. 'Mrs Musbury, the widow who lives on the other side of Softly's Bottom. Striking looking woman. Always wears a hat. She could talk the hind leg off a donkey.'

'Oh that Mrs Musbury!' exclaimed Peter, as though the village were awash with Mrs Musburys. He thought for a moment. 'Do you know I think you could be right. I'll pop round this afternoon and have a word with her. Do you think she'd take the job without a salary? Just a commission on every house she sells?'

'You could try,' I told him. 'I rather think she'd like the job. It would give her a chance to go in and out of everyone's house and measure every available bathroom.'

I left Peter rubbing his hands with delight at the thought of signing up the first employee for his burgeoning estate agency.

I drove back to Bilbury Grange, had my lunch, did a couple more visits, sat in the garden and wrote a few words for the Bilbury book I was working on, and then it was time for the evening surgery.

It was only when I sat down behind my surgery desk that I realised that I had been so busy that I hadn't had the time to have a cup of tea and a couple of digestive biscuits.

To my astonishment, Mrs Musbury was the first patient to enter. I was startled because she had acquired a habit of hanging back so that she could be the last patient and stay for a long chat.

'I can't stop long, doctor,' she said, entering the surgery in a rush. 'But I did say I'd call in this evening and I thought I ought to just drop by and tell you that I won't be able to pop in quite as often as before.'

'Oh dear,' I said, feigning a little (but not too much) disappointment.

'Mr Marshall has appointed me the new general manager of his estate agency,' she announced with great pride and in something of a rush. 'And he wants me to go round this evening to help him plan the business. So I'll have to be on my way. We're going to have a brainstorming session while we do something together with crossword books.'

'Congratulations!' I said. I couldn't help congratulating myself on my newfound matchmaking skills. 'So, Peter is going into the real estate business is he?' I don't know why but I didn't want Mrs Musbury to know that I'd suggested her for the job.

'Oh yes!' said Mrs Musbury. 'Isn't it exciting? It will be Bilbury's first estate agency. And I'm to be the general manager. Mr Marshall is going to print up some visiting cards for me.'

'Marvellous,' I agreed.

'If you ever decide to put Bilbury Grange on the market you will think of me, won't you?' She looked around the room as though measuring it up ready to write the particulars.

'Of course,' I agreed. 'But Patsy and I don't have any plans to sell the house.'

'You wouldn't like me to just wander around and measure up?' she asked. 'Just in case you change your minds?'

'No thank you. I don't think so.'

'You have very nice mullion windows. Quite a feature, I've often thought. A very sought after element in a property. Do the fireplaces all work?'

'Thank you. You've very kind. Yes, they do.'

'Well, I'd better be off. If you know anyone who does want to sell their home you make sure they get in touch with me straight away. I'll bring in a few of my cards when they're ready.'

I thanked her but it seemed that the sudden storm was over and Mrs Musbury was half way out of the room.

Just then, the door opened and Patsy appeared holding a cup of tea. There were, I was delighted to see, two digestive biscuits in the saucer.

'Is that for me, dear?' said Mrs Musbury, eyeing up the tea. 'That's very sweet of you but I'm afraid I don't have the time. I have to hurry off to a business meeting.'

'That's all right,' replied Patsy, not missing a beat. 'I'm sure the doctor will be happy to drink it.' She walked across and put the tea down on my desk.

'I won't be able to come in as often as before,' Mrs Musbury said to Patsy. 'I've taken a position under Mr Marshall. I expect your husband will miss our little chats.'

'Oh, I'm sure he will!' said Patsy.

And then Mrs Musbury was gone.

'A position under Mr Marshall?' said Patsy, raising a querulous eyebrow. 'Did she really say that?'

'I'll explain later,' I assured her. 'It's probably not as exciting as it sounds.'

I picked up one of the digestive biscuits and dunked it gently into the cup of tea.

'Do you remember the character played by Barry Fitzgerald in *The Quiet Man*?'

'The matchmaker who brought John Wayne and Maureen O'Hara together?'

'That's the one,' I confirmed. 'Well, that's me, now. I'm the Bilbury matchmaker.'

'You haven't set Peter Marshall up with Hilda Musbury!'

'Only in a business sort of way.'

'That sounds even worse.'

'I'll explain later,' I repeated.

'You'd better!' said Patsy.

The Parisians

I was sitting in the snug at the Duck and Puddle.

My companions were Thumper Robinson, poacher, dealer and general fixer upper, Patchy Fogg, antiques dealer, and Frank Parsons, our ever genial landlord. Thumper had his usual pint of Old Restoration. Patchy was drinking a glass of Jack Daniels. Frank was sipping a small glass of port (his intake of alcohol is strictly regulated by his wife). And I was nursing a glass of an 18-year-old malt whisky called Tullibardine.

We sit at the same table, in the same places, and get quite upset if Gilly Parsons changes the beermats too often. What is wrong with comfort and routine?

There can be no doubt that our conversations are always intellectual, always provocative and always illuminating. I like to think of us as the natural descendants of the literati who favoured the famous table at the Algonquin Hotel in New York.

Outside Bilbury, the world rushes along like an out of control Express train; forever whistling and screaming and jumping off the tracks. And it seems to me that most of the alleged progress on offer produces little more than noise, confusion, frustration and disappointment. Indeed, much of what passes for progress is little more than a nod in the direction of fashion for although we think of fashion as merely affecting hemlines and button configuration, it invades far more of our lives than that. In Bilbury, we like to move along at a more sedate pace; accepting such items of progress which promise to make our lives better in some way.

But then, that's why I like Bilbury and I recognise that our leisurely pace of life would not suit everyone.

'You've got a bit of competition in the making-people-better business,' said Thumper.

I looked at him, surprised to hear this. I hadn't heard of any other doctor setting up in the village.

'Someone called a complementary health specialist has opened up a clinic in Combe Martin,' said Thumper. 'Anne found a leaflet pushed half-way through our letterbox.'

'Like the little sachets of shampoo and soap you get in posh hotels?' asked Frank.

We all looked at him.

'Complimentary,' explained Frank. 'They're complimentary. It means you don't have to pay for them.' He paused for a moment and then a puzzled and worried look appeared on his face. 'But we don't pay you, do we?' he said to me. 'The National Health Service is free.'

'The NHS isn't really free,' I pointed out. 'It's paid for out of taxes.'

'Oh, is it?' said Frank, with a shudder. 'I don't have anything to do with any of that stuff. Those chaps in grey suits come round occasionally and Gilly shows them the books and they look at her pityingly and go away shaking their heads and muttering.'

I noticed that Thumper was examining his glass of beer very carefully; in the manner of a man who is pretending to be elsewhere; studying one thing in an effort to make it clear that he has nothing whatsoever to do with another.

I have noticed the same thing with our cats.

If they fall off a piece of furniture, or knock a vase off a shelf, they will instantly start cleaning themselves, making it abundantly clear that they have nothing to do with whatever may have happened in the vicinity.

'Oh, gosh, has a vase jumped off the mantelpiece? How shocking! Me? No, I didn't see anything.'

I happen to know that Thumper, like Frank, doesn't pay any tax. I'm not even sure that the authorities know he exists these days. He had an unfortunate encounter with the constabulary a few years ago when there was a slight misunderstanding involving a river, half a dozen trout and a 'missing' licence and he has, since then, kept a low profile as far as the authorities are concerned.

'It's not that sort of 'complimentary',' said Patchy. He looked at me, waiting for me to say something. But I just smiled at him.

Frank looked at him and thought for a while. 'What other sort is there?'

'Well, there's the sort when you tell Gilly that her hair looks nice and you like her hat,' said Thumper, looking up and returning to the conversation. He spoke with the quiet but slightly surprising confidence of a man who can tickle a trout and tease a pheasant out of a thicket but who has never seen a dictionary, let alone consulted one.

Frank stared at him and frowned. When Frank frowns it usually means that he's thinking hard. 'I don't think I've ever seen Gilly in a hat,' he said at last.

'She wore a hat to our wedding,' I reminded him. 'It was a very smart one; a big white one which had a large brim. It had a yellow ribbon, a huge bow and lots of flowers. I seem to remember that there were half a dozen red cherries on it too.' The ladies of Bilbury like cherries on their hats. Patsy's mum has a hat which is festooned with a whole bunch of cherries.

'Oh yes, I remember,' said Frank. He laughed. Frank has a wonderful deep laugh, created by years of smoking cigars and cigarettes and drinking rough liquor.

Patchy looked around nervously, making sure that Gilly wasn't within earshot. He knew that she wouldn't have liked the idea of Frank laughing at her hat.

'It was a splendid hat!' I said, defending Gilly's choice of headgear. Ever the gentleman.

'Someone sat on it and crushed it,' remembered Frank. 'I mended it with some sticky tape and then it blew off and we never saw it again.'

'It was Patsy's Aunt Edna from Cornwall,' I said, remembering the incident. 'She doesn't have terribly good eyesight. She said she thought it was a cushion.'

'I think I saw it on a scarecrow in a field just outside Parracombe,' said Thumper. 'It wasn't quite so white but it still had most of the flowers. It was definitely Gilly's hat.'

Frank looked shocked. 'Don't for heaven's sake tell Gilly.' He shuddered. 'So that's what this complimentary medicine is all about then? You tell them they're looking good and you like their hat? It doesn't sound much like medicine to me.'

I felt I ought to say something and so I started to explain precisely what the phrase 'complementary medicine' really means. But Thumper was determined to say something and spoke over me.

'I'd bet it works well,' said Thumper, speaking with enthusiasm. 'I remember there was a song when I was a kid. It was sung by Stanley Holloway, the chap who played the dustman in *My Fair Lady*. There was this one chap who had been ill and was feeling much brighter. He went for a walk and kept meeting people who said to him 'My word, you do look queer'. The result was that the poor fellow became depressed and decided that he was finished. Then up came one final fellow who said to him 'My word you do look well!' That's all it took. The chap who was feeling down was so cheered by this that he suddenly felt full of life. In the song he decided that 'There's life in the old dog yet'. So there you: complimentary medicine can work!'

I tried once more to speak. But this time it was Patchy who spoke.

'I can see that it would work,' said Patchy. 'Saying something nice to a person always makes them feel better. Congratulate them on a nice tie or hairdo and you're bound to make them feel better.'

I was confident that Patchy knew the difference between complimentary medicine and complementary medicine but to be honest I wasn't so sure about Thumper and I was pretty sure that Frank didn't suspect that there was any difference at all. And so I didn't make another effort to contradict anyone. It seemed a pity to spoil the fun.

Indeed, I rather hoped that Thumper and Frank would one day be able to use their new knowledge somewhere else.

'Do you think that maybe this complimentary person lets you eat and drink as much as you like?' Frank asked me.

Frank had had a stroke, caused by high blood pressure, and he had, for some time, been on a diet as well as having his alcohol consumption strictly controlled. I had made the rules but Gilly enforced them.

'I'm afraid I rather doubt it,' I told him. 'They'll probably want you to eat a good deal of seaweed while they stick needles into you.'

Frank managed to look startled and not a little disappointed at the same time. It is not often that Frank manages to do two things at once.

Just then, the door swung open and two visitors walked in. It was clearly still raining outside for the minute they entered the snug they both stood for a moment and shook themselves, like dogs who've just had a swim. I don't think any of us had noticed that it was still raining. The truth is that it rains a good deal in North Devon and we only really notice the weather when it isn't raining.

The visitors were wearing waterproof trousers, waterproof jackets, waterproof hats and boots that were also doubtless waterproof. Everything they wore was shiny with water. It was difficult to be certain but it seemed likely that one of the visitors was equipped with two X chromosomes while the other was having to make do with one.

'Good morning!' said the taller of the two visitors. 'We would like to purchase provender at your café. We wish first to divest ourselves of our vestments.' He unzipped his jacket as he spoke.

Frank, who is always a welcoming and genial host, got up from his chair and strolled over to where the two newcomers were standing. I would have bet a month's income that he didn't have the faintest idea what they were talking about but he showed no sign of failing to understand them. 'Hang your gear on the hat stand,' he said, pointing to a huge brass coat rack which stands in a corner of the snug. Come far?'

'Yes, please,' said the shorter of the two. 'We have come for comestibles.'

This was clearly going to be fun.

The two strangers removed their waterproofs and hung them on the coat rack. The man had a bit of a struggle with his and the zip on his jacket caught in the jumper he was wearing underneath. Water dripped from every item and soaked into the carpet. If Gilly had been around she would have made them leave their soaking gear in the porch.

Underneath their waterproofs, they were dressed identically. They both wore blue jeans and red sweaters. I noticed that their jeans and sweaters both appeared to be soaked. The battle with the elements in North Devon had clearly been lost.

The two of them were much smaller than they had appeared to be in their waterproofs. They were both very slim and they looked to be in their late 20s. She had very short hair. He had shoulder length hair.

The man examined his jumper where it had been snagged by the zip. 'I'll get a pair of scissors and cut that off for you,' said Frank, kindly. He tottered over to the bar, returned with a pair of scissors and snipped off the offending piece of wool. The man did not say anything but accepted this service without thanks.

For no reason whatsoever, I found myself wondering why we refer to scissors as being a pair. It's like trousers, spectacles and binoculars. It makes sense to talk of a pair of shoes or a pair of socks because there are two of them. But why do scissors, trousers, spectacles and binoculars always come as pairs? It really doesn't make any sense since none of them is a paired items in the sense that two matching candlesticks can be described as a pair; a set of two things used together and regarded as a unit.

I have these thoughts quite often and I worry about myself sometimes. Still, I try to keep the thoughts to myself.

'You wish to drink, yes?' said Frank. 'And eat food?' He picked up an imaginary glass and took an imaginary gulp from it. He then mimed eating a sandwich.

In addition to the Marcel Marceau impersonation, he had, I noticed, raised his voice since he knew he was speaking to foreigners and he wanted to make it easier for them to understand what he was saying.

'Where are you from?' asked Patchy, speaking very slowly. He too spoke a little louder than usual.

'We are coming out of Lynmouth,' said the woman. 'We are heading into Ilfracombe.'

'A walking voyage,' said the man.

It seemed to me that, judging by the weather, the word 'voyage' was probably appropriate. It also occurred to me that they were slightly mad. The distance between Lynmouth and Ilfracombe is at least 20 miles. And since they were now undeniably in Bilbury, it was pretty clear that, either by design or accident, they weren't taking the direct route.

'No, I meant, what country are you from?' said Patchy.

'From France, of course,' said the woman, as though it were a stupid question. 'We are habituated at Paris.'

'Ah,' said Frank, nodding wisely. 'You are French?'

'Yes!' said the man, as though he were talking to an idiot. 'Of course we are French.'

'You speak very good English,' lied Patchy.

In England we always do that. When a foreigner speaks our language we always congratulate them and tell them how well they speak it. I don't why this is. If we meet someone who knows three words of English we pretend to be astounded and tell them how fluent they are. This, of course, gives them false confidence and in the end usually results in misunderstandings, confusion, bewilderment, disappointment and, quite often, a few tears.

'Oh yes,' said the woman. 'We are beyond dispute talking in the perfect English.'

'What can I get you to drink?' asked Frank. He made the drinking sign again.

'We would desire to be quaffing coffee,' said the woman.

'Coffee?' said a rather startled Frank, for whom coffee is something to be drunk after a meal and not as an alternative to alcohol. He had probably expected the woman to order a bottle of wine to drink while they decided what to have to drink.

'Coffee,' agreed the woman.

'Both of you?'

'I beg your pardon?'

'You both want coffee?' Frank pointed at the woman and then at the man.

'Yes,' said the woman, rather impatiently. 'Do you have a carte?'

Frank looked puzzled. 'No,' he said, 'but Thumper has an old truck.'

'A carte,' repeated the woman. 'A directory of your foods.' She looked at her companion and raised an eyebrow. I got the impression they both wished they had chosen to eat somewhere else. Since the Duck and Puddle is the only eating establishment for miles in any direction, this was a pointless regret.

'Oh, you mean a menu!' said Frank, understanding at last.

'Yes. A menus. Are you having one of those?'

'I bet they'll want snails,' whispered Thumper to me. 'If they do I could easily pop outside and collect a few dozen.' Thumper's version of sotto voce is most people's idea of a full throated roar.

'No, not at the moment,' admitted Frank in response to the menu question. 'We did have one. Well, actually we had three. But one fell into the fire, one was stolen by a tourist and I can't find the other one. But it doesn't matter because I know what we've got.'

'Do you have any crudités?' asked the woman.

'No, no,' said Frank looking shocked. 'This isn't that sort of place. We're a family pub. Very old fashioned. No entertainment. No crudities.'

'She means chopped vegetables,' I murmured to Frank. 'Crudites is a French dish. Raw vegetables sliced and served with some sort of sauce.'

Frank looked at me. 'Raw vegetables?'

I nodded. 'Raw.'

'Bloody hell,' said Frank with his own version of sotto voce. 'They eat raw veggies? No wonder the Froggies always lose every damned war they fight.'

'What is that?' asked the French woman.

'Mon ami a dit qu'il pleut beaucoup aujourdhui,' said Patchy, with a big smile. The smile he usually reserves for the moment when he's closing on a deal to sell Shakespeare's writing desk to a gullible tourist. 'My friend said that it rains a good deal today.'

'Your pronunciations en Francais are not very up to the marker,' said the woman with a very superior and quite natural sneer. She turned to her companion. 'The English, like the Americans, never well speak the langue,' she said to him, with a Gallic shrug of her damp shoulders.

The Frenchman curled a lip in attempted disdain.

It occurred to me that apart from Elvis Presley, who has always done it with great charm, I've never seen anyone do that successfully. Lip curling is obviously an acquired skill.

In the interests of international relations, and out of a sense of wild adventure, I had been preparing to share with them the knowledge that my uncle's pen resides in the bureau of my aunt but I decided to keep this knowledge to myself, and to hide my own multilingual light under a bushel. I had, to be honest, thought Patchy's accent to be pretty good. But then, in my experience, the French like to think that they are the only people who can speak their language properly and will criticise foreigners whatever they say and however they say it.

I long ago learned never to say 'yes' when I am asked by a Frenchman (or Frenchwoman) if I speak French. It is much better to force them to rack their brains trying to speak English. They will invariably become confused, lose control of the conversation and provide considerable amusement.

Frank and Gilly once had a French fellow staying at the Duck and Puddle. He was on a tour of West Country follies (there are many) and on his first night at the pub he announced that he would like a 'night hat'. Frank, ever helpful, said they didn't have one of those traditional caps to lend him but he could provide a woollen watch cap with a bobble on the top as an alternative.

When the Frenchman seemed surprised by this, we all tried alternative suggestions.

Patchy even went back home and fetched his Sherlock Holmes style deerstalker in case the fellow wanted to keep his ears warm.

In the end, it turned out that the chap wanted a 'night cap' rather than a 'night hat'.

I remember that the fellow was quite humourless, as most of the French are, and very full of his own sense of importance, as they tend to be.

I remember he told us repeatedly that he was due to have dinner with the county's Lord Lieutenant, and Patchy, rather fed up with the name dropping, told him that when meeting the British aristocracy it is the usual practice to bow slightly, click your heels and say: 'Watcha cock, how are they hanging.'

We still like to think that he followed Patchy's advice.

The funny thing is, of course, that although they like to criticise us when we try to speak French, those French folk who speak a word or two of English always believe they are fluent.

Patchy once pointed out to me that no Frenchman has ever learned to speak English properly, though they all think they have. Out of politeness, we never tell them that they're making zillions of mistakes every time they open their mouths. They tell us if we get a tense or a conjugation or a pronunciation slightly wrong. But we never tell them because we are too damned polite.

But, as Patchy says, the French are quite nice sometimes, when you consider that they live on a diet of onions, snails, smelly cheeses and frogs' legs.

'I could get you a raw vegetable if that's what you want,' said Frank. 'What would you like? A potato? I could cut up a raw potato into little pieces and serve you raw chips if you like. Or a carrot? A cabbage? A whole cabbage would be a bit much, perhaps. The ones we've got at the moment are quite big. Maybe half a cabbage? Or how about a nice plateful of Brussels sprouts? They named them after Brussels and that isn't far from France is it? Or is it in France? I can never remember. It's certainly foreign. So, perhaps you'd like half a dozen raw sprouts? Maybe with a little tomato sauce? Or we've got brown sauce? Both sorts: Daddy's and HP.'

You have to give Frank points for attempting to be helpful. But when he gets a little agitated, Frank tends to lose control of his brain. I had an awful feeling that he was going to serve up a whole, raw potato on a plate. Or, perhaps, bring in half a dozen Brussels sprouts covered in HP sauce. Wars have probably been fought over less.

But, fortunately, this wasn't going to happen. The French woman screwed up her nose and looked at her companion. He shook his head. 'Not on your Nellie,' he said.

It took us all quite a while to realise what he'd said. Frank was shocked and rather upset. He doesn't like rude people and saying 'Not on your Nellie' when your host has been bending over backwards to meet your peculiar dietary requirements is, in our book, definitely on the rude side of polite.

'I can do you a sandwich,' said Frank, through gritted teeth. 'Cheese, ham, beef or tomato and salady stuff.' Frank is not a fan of what he calls 'salady stuff'. He regards lettuce as being an unsuitable food for a human being.

'Do you have the Roquefort?'

'Is that the smelly goat cheese?'

'It is being made from the milk of the goat, yes.'

'No.'

'You are not having this one?'

'No.'

'You are having the Camembert?'

'No.'

'The Brie?'

'No.'

'What do you have?' The question was asked with a sneer of gladiatorial proportions.

'The Cheddar.'

The Frenchman screwed up his nose in distaste. 'You are having only the Cheddar?'

'Yes. Only the Cheddar.'

Frank would serve the man because he was a customer and customers are there to be served. But he would now not be polite to him. Serving food to customers is Frank's job. He doesn't believe there is a rule that he has to be nice to them if he doesn't like them.

'Pouf! The Cheddar is for mices,' said the Frenchman, screwing up his nose in disgust.

'I'll go and feed the mices then,' said Frank, who had had enough. 'You pair can bugger off.' And with that he turned on his heel and disappeared.

'I will take the ham sandwich,' said the Frenchman, addressing us. 'With a cappuccino with extra milk.' He turned to his companion who thought for a while. 'I'll have the same,' she said at last. She sniffed and did not seem very happy.

'Afraid not, mate,' said Thumper. 'You've upset the landlord and he's gone. But there's a shop in the village and the bloke there will sell you a couple of packets of crisps and a can of something fizzy.'

The couple stared at us in disbelief.

'We are not to be a serving?' she said, astonished.

'Doesn't look like it,' said Thumper. 'No Frank, no food is the general rule here. He always allows foreigners a little extra leeway, on account of the language and so on, but I think you overstepped the mark with that remark about the mices.'

'Huh!' said the Frenchman. 'What is this with the 'foreigner'? Huh! In France you would be the foreigner.'

Thumper laughed. 'Don't be daft, sunbeam' he said. 'There's no way I could ever be a foreigner. I'm English!'

Empty of food but full of indignation, the French folk struggled back into their waterproofs and headed back out into the rain.

They discovered, I am sure, that it is not easy to be dignified when climbing back into still damp waterproofs.

'Toodle pip,' said Thumper, as they left.

The woman turned back, blank faced and bewildered. 'What is this 'toodle pip'?' she demanded.

'Oh, it's English, love,' replied Thumper. 'You wouldn't understand. You being foreign.'

The woman followed her companion and tried to slam the door. Unfortunately, the door she tried to slam had a powerful spring attached to it and cannot be slammed.

'I'm never going to bother trying to speak French again,' muttered Patchy. 'They can speak English like proper, educated, civilised people do. The Americans speak English, the Canadians speak English, the New Zealanders speak English, even the Australians speak a type of English. Why do the French insist on speaking their own funny little language?'

Thumper and I laughed rather nervously. Patchy can sometimes get a trifle upset if people are rude to him.

'If you make an effort to speak their language,' said Patchy, 'the French will criticise everything you say. They will delight in picking holes in your grammar and they will constantly correct your pronunciation. And what's the point? If you speak French to a Frenchman you will always be searching for the appropriate word. You will be forever on the back foot, struggling to make sure that you aren't making a mistake which will result in your listener collapsing to the floor and holding his stomach as he struggles to contain his laughter.' Patchy made a passable imitation of a stage Frenchman laughing. He did sound a bit like Maurice Chevalier. 'On the other hand, if he has to try to speak your language you can chuckle merrily and raise eyebrows occasionally. So I shall insist on having all my future conversations in English, putting the French person on the back foot. They will have to put a lot of effort into struggling to cope with a foreign language and they will have less brain available to deal with the problem at hand. And I shall destabilise them by constantly correcting their English. I shall distribute idioms at random and when correcting a foreigner who is attempting to speak 'the English' I shall always appear to be understanding and patronising. I shall tell them they are doing really well and I shall ask them if they learned their English at school. If they seem fluent, I shall ask them how many weeks they have been learning English. This will doubtless make them feel inferior and intimidated and will drive them insane. I shall pretend not to understand what they are saying. If they say 'I am unhappy with the gilding on this frame', I shall reply 'I'm sorry, did you say you want to wrap the picture so that you can take it away with you now?''

Thumper and I looked at each other and then at Patchy.

'Finished?' I said.

Patchy sat back, smiled and nodded. 'I feel better now.'

There was something close to silence for a while. Only the crackling of the fire and the sound of the rain on the windows could be heard.

'All that talk of food has made me peckish,' said Thumper, breaking the silence at last.

'Me too,' I agreed.

'Frank!' called Patchy, who had recovered completely now and clearly felt better after his rant. 'Don't give the Cheddar to the mice. We'll have three large cheese and onion sandwiches and another round of drinks.'

I got up and put a log on the fire. It was very wet and cold outside and the wind was now howling with slate tearing determination. For a moment, I wondered how much guttering we would lose at Bilbury Grange. But only for a moment. The vicious winds which scour the North Devon coast are an integral part of our lives and a small price to pay for living in such a beautiful and deserted part of England.

I wondered how the couple from Paris were getting on, out there in the rain and the wind.

It was warm and cosy in the Duck and Puddle snug.

Mind you, it is always warm and cosy in the snug at the Duck and Puddle.

The False Widow

It is a fact of mechanical life that all motor cars have their off days and it is, I suppose, not unreasonable to suspect that a motor car built in the early 1930s, and well on its way to its first half century, would probably be more vulnerable to the work of gremlins than any other mechanical device, particularly one built within the last few years.

It is also a fact of life that when things go wrong with anything mechanical, they usually do so at the most inconvenient moment.

This is, I suppose, inevitable, in that when, for example, a motor car breaks down the driver is, by definition, always trying to get somewhere, and to be somewhere that he isn't, when the breakdown takes place.

This is rather similar to the inconvenience of a light bulb going 'pop' when you press the 'on' switch. When you try to turn on a light, you are doing so because it is dark and you need the light. You are always going into another room or about to do something which requires light. So light bulbs always 'go' at an inconvenient moment.

But sometimes, it does seem as though fate is having a laugh.

The Rolls Royce 20/25 which I had inherited from my predecessor, Dr Brownlow, had always been entirely reliable. Indeed, I took her reliability for granted. And I was, therefore, enormously surprised when she broke down for the first time since she had been in my possession.

Naturally, I was out on a night call when she let me down.

There was no moon so it was pitch black. The nearest street lights to Bilbury are the ones in Wales, on the other side of the Bristol Channel and the village is, therefore, entirely reliant upon the heavens for all illumination.

There was no visible moon and no stars and, therefore, no illumination.

And it goes without saying that it was raining.

It was, indeed, raining with so much enthusiasm that it appeared as if the sky must have found itself with several hundred thousand tons of excess water which had to be got rid of as quickly as possible.

The call I was answering had sounded urgent and in my rush, I had gone out without a raincoat or a hat. I had simply slipped an old sweater and a pair of trousers over the top of my pyjamas.

And, to make things even worse, the call was to a house which was several miles away from Bilbury Grange. The house to which I had been called wasn't actually even in Bilbury but was in a small hamlet called East Morton, several miles away.

I didn't have any patients in East Morton but the caller had stated that her husband was ill, that they were staying in a house, called The Castle, which they had rented and that their own doctor was in Harley Street. The woman who called told me that she had given my name and telephone number by their live-in butler. He wasn't a patient of mine either and I never did find out why he chose to recommend me to his mistress.

I know nothing whatsoever about motor cars and when the Rolls spluttered to a halt, I had absolutely no idea what to do. There was no point in my lifting the bonnet. Indeed, although I am rather ashamed to admit it, I didn't even know how to lift the bonnet.

So, when it was clear that the car wasn't going to respond to my attempts to restart it I picked up my black medical bag, climbed out into the rain and started the long trudge along the lanes to East Morton.

Naturally, I discovered that the torch I kept in the car had a flat battery.

Isn't it always the way?

The small pen torch which I use to look down patients' throats was the only illumination I had and although its tiny beam was absolutely fine for examining tonsils, it turned out to be utterly useless for helping me find my way along the Devon lanes.

After trudging along for a quarter of a mile, I was totally soaked. My hair was plastered to my head and my jumper and trousers were drenched. In my haste to get up and out, I had slipped my feet into a pair of canvas deck shoes. I kept them ready for night calls because they were quicker to put on than decent, sturdy shoes which required lacing. The deck shoes too were soaked and kept slipping off my feet as I made my way along the now muddy lanes. And still the rain came down.

After around half a mile, I lost a shoe.

I stopped for a while to hunt for it but eventually gave up and plodded on without it. The lanes in that part of the world are rough and uneven and the puddles which form are consequently huge. I've seen smaller garden ponds.

A little further along the road, I stumbled in a pothole and fell sideways into a water filled ditch. In a way, it didn't really matter because I was already as wet as I could get but I ripped a huge hole in my jumper as I scrambled out and caught a sleeve on a huge bramble.

Instead of just being bedraggled, I was now wet and bedraggled. And still the rain came down.

When I finally arrived in the hamlet of East Morton, I realised that I didn't have the foggiest idea where to find The Castle. I walked round and round the lanes, desperately peering at gateposts and the front doors of the odd cottage. The night was so dark and the rain so heavy that I had to get within a couple of feet of a sign to see what it said.

At this point, I was feeling very sorry for myself and I honestly wanted to just sit down on the lane and give up.

But I persevered.

Eventually, I came across a gateway guarded by two stone pillars, both of which bore the name The Castle carved into stone blocks. Inevitably, the driveway was long and lined with horse chestnut trees. By now, the wind had joined the party and the air was thick with leaves and small branches which had been torn from the trees. I'm sure that in the daylight, sitting in a comfortable motor car or carriage, the driveway would have looked imposing and stylish but in the rain and the wind the darned driveway simply seemed interminable.

Somewhere along the drive, I lost my one remaining shoe.

Since I hadn't bothered to waste time putting on any socks before I left the house, I was now barefoot. Every now and then I trod on a sharp stone. I did a good deal of yelping. On one occasion, I shouted rude words at the top of my voice. Sadly, no one heard them for my words were lost on the wind.

The house, when I finally got there, was large and imposing and looked as if it would make a good film set for a horror film. I couldn't see the extent of it but it seemed vast; stretching to left and right as far as I could see in the darkness of that foul night. It was the sort of house which has a gun room, a game larder, a flower room and a wrapping room. My night vision had improved by now and my pupils must have been enormous. I found the front door, discovered the door bell and pushed a huge porcelain button marked 'Bell'. While I waited for someone to answer, I looked at my watch. It was 1.30 am. I had set out from Bilbury Grange just before midnight.

'Yes?' said the large and imposing man who opened the door. He was wearing evening dress and looked as if he had been dusted and polished.

'I'm the doctor,' I explained. 'I've forgotten who telephoned me but I was asked to call.'

'You're the doctor?' said the man. It occurred to me that he must have been the butler.

I told him my name and realised that I was shivering. I was drenched to the skin. My hair was plastered to my head. My jumper was unravelling. And I was standing there in bare feet. But I was holding a black medical bag. If I hadn't been holding the bag I think he would have just shut the door on me.

'My car broke down,' I explained. 'I had to walk.' I looked down. 'I lost my shoes somewhere along the way.'

The butler opened the door wide and stood aside to give me room to enter.

'Who is it, Beddowes?' demanded an imperious voice belonging to an invisible woman.

'It's a person who says he is a doctor, madam,' said the butler.

The owner of the voice appeared. She was wearing an evening dress and holding a glass of champagne. She looked to be in her 50s but I suppose she could have been older.

'You're the doctor?' she said, making little effort to hide her disbelief and contempt.

'Yes,' I said.

'You've taken your time,' she said.

'My car broke down,' I explained.

'You should have something a little more reliable,' was her answer.

'It's usually very reliable,' I said, defending my car's reputation.

'You're dripping wet.'

'It's raining.'

'Don't you have a coat you could have worn? Or an umbrella?'

'Not with me, no,' I said. I wanted to say that if I had a coat I would have been wearing it. And that if I'd had an umbrella I would have used it. But she wasn't the sort of woman who takes it kindly when the help speaks back. I couldn't help feeling rather intimidated. I hate it when I feel intimidated. I hate the person intimidating me and I despise myself for being intimidated. 'Where's my patient?'

The woman looked me up and down. 'I'll take you to him,' she said. 'But try not to walk on the carpets. You are dripping wet and your feet are filthy.'

I looked down. My feet were very grubby. And I was standing in the middle of a puddle which I had created. I was about to take off my jumper when I realised that all I had on underneath it was my pyjama jacket. It occurred to me that it might have been kind of her to have offered to lend me a towel. Or even some dry clothing. I knew that poorer patients living in a run-down cottage would have definitely offered me towels and a dressing gown.

'Sir Felix was taken very poorly this afternoon,' said the woman as she led the way down a long corridor. As instructed, I walked on the wooden floor at the side of the carpet. 'I couldn't telephone you until after dinner because we had very important guests. Lord Braunton and Sir Percy Liverage were here.'

'What are Sir Felix's symptoms?' I asked. I had never heard of Lord Braunton or Sir Percy Liverage and didn't give a fig for them. We were now making our way up a very impressive marble staircase. The carpet stretched from one side of the staircase so I had no choice but to walk on it. However, my feet were not quite as dirty as they had been. And I was no longer dripping water like a tap turned full on. I wondered if the woman I was following was Sir Felix's wife.

'I expect he'll want to tell you that himself,' said the woman. She turned left at the top of the stairs and led me along another corridor. This one was long enough for an archery contest.

She stopped at last and knocked on a door. There were no numbers or other identifying marks on any of the doors so I have no idea how she knew that this was the correct door.

'This man says he is the doctor,' said the woman, standing to one side to let me past.

We were in a bedroom.

The sole occupant was a large, red-faced man who was sitting up in bed reading a newspaper. He was wearing spectacles perched on the end of his nose and looked very bad tempered. There were a dozen suitcases stacked up against one wall. The suitcases all carried the Louis Vuitton brand markings. The man looked up and peered at me over the tops of his spectacles.

'He says his car broke down and that it is raining,' said the woman to the red-faced man. It was clearly offered as an explanation for my appearance.

The man in bed examined me and glowered as though I were a sick animal and he were deciding whether or not to have me put down. 'You're late and you look very disreputable,' he said. 'We rang for you hours ago.'

'I'm sorry,' I said, for I was.

'Damned good job I'm not dying,' said the man. 'What if I'd been dying, eh?'

'I couldn't get here any quicker,' I apologised. 'You're actually well outside my practice area.'

'Then you shouldn't have come.'

'I was asked to come,' I replied, feeling rather cross. 'What's the problem?' I put my black bag down on a chair near to the bed.

'That's what you're here for,' snapped the man. 'No good asking me what the problem is. If I were the doctor I'd know and I'd deal with it. But I'm not.' He had a discomforting way of looking through me – as though he were looking at something a foot behind my head. It was very intimidating and I felt certain that he was doing it on purpose.

I tried again. 'What symptoms have you got?'

'Aching, sweating, shaky,' he replied. 'Nauseous. I feel awful. Tired and washed out. Not usually like this at all.'

I opened my bag and took out my stethoscope and my sphygmomanometer. The rain had somehow got into my bag and everything inside was soaked. His heart was a little fast and his blood pressure was a little high but I couldn't find anything else wrong. I started to pull back the heavy eiderdown and the sheets beneath it.

'What on earth are you doing?' screamed the woman who had brought me to the bedroom. I still didn't know who she was but in my innocence I thought it was a fair bet that since he was Sir Felix something then she was probably Lady something.

'I need to examine Sir Felix,' I explained. 'I can't do it while he's covered up.'

'Wait!' ordered the woman. 'I'll call for someone.' She rang a bell by the door. A minute or two later a woman in a black uniform arrived. She looked to be the wrong side of 50 and had the put-upon stoop of a woman whose life is not and never has been her own and who is accustomed to taking orders without thought. I wondered if the poor woman had to stay up until her master and mistress went to bed, just in case they needed something. I'd never seen her or the butler before.

'Turn down the bedspread so that the doctor can examine Sir Felix,' said the woman.

'Sir Felix's pyjamas are soaked,' I said. 'He has been sweating rather a lot. He needs some fresh ones.'

When the bedspread had been properly turned down (so neatly that I half expected to see a neatly wrapped chocolate placed on the pillow just as they do in posh hotels) the woman giving the orders pointed to the suitcases. 'Look in those,' she said to the woman in the black uniform. 'You'll find new pyjamas in one of them.' She turned to me. 'We're only down here for the week,' she explained. 'We did some shopping in Monaco and brought some stuff with us but there hasn't been time for the staff to unpack yet.'

I examined Sir Felix.

I couldn't find anything wrong with him except for some purple, puffy patches on the skin of his left foot. There was also a raised area around a tiny bite.

'Ah, forgot to tell you about that skin thing,' he said. 'Rather clever of you to find it. The bite thing burns like stink. I've also had a stabbing pain up my leg.'

'It looks like a bite,' I said.

'It was. I was putting on my boots to take the dogs for a walk and I was bitten. I looked inside my boot and there was a damned spider there. It bit my foot.' He was clearly still shocked that anyone or anything should dare to bite him.

'What sort of spider was it? Did you recognise it?'

'Damned stupid question,' said Sir Felix. 'I'm not on first name terms with all the spiders in the house. There are thousands of them around – especially when it rains.'

I noticed, out of the corner of my eye, that the woman in the black uniform had now opened six or seven suitcases. She was being supervised by the woman who had shown me up into the bedroom. The contents of the suitcases, all clothes, were all brand new and still wrapped in cellophane or tissue paper. Some were still in the carrier bags in which the shops had sold them. There did not appear to be any sign of any pyjamas. It was clear that none of the clothes had ever been worn. Blazers, jackets, suits, dresses, evening gowns, shirts, trousers – there was enough clothing there to stock an expensive store. I got the impression that Sir Felix and his lady rather liked shopping. It was all like something out of an Edwardian drama; the curmudgeonly old man, the immaculate butler, the snooty woman and the put upon maidservant. It was difficult to believe that this was England in the 1970s.

'No, of course not,' I apologised, 'I'm sorry; I meant to ask if you recognised the type of spider.'

'Are there different types of spider?' he asked. He thought for a moment. 'I suppose there are,' he admitted. 'This was one of the little ones with a big body and short legs rather than one of those with a tiny body and long legs.'

'How big would you say?'

'Small. The whole thing was no bigger than my little fingernail. Some white markings on the body and I seem to remember that it had orangish legs.'

'You should address Sir Felix as Sir Felix,' interrupted the bossy woman.

I looked at her. I was getting fed up with the rather feudal atmosphere in the house. 'And I should be addressed as 'doctor',' I told her.

I'm delighted to say that she went bright red.

I looked closely at the skin around the bite. Although Sir Felix had been sweating profusely, the area of skin around the bite was quite dry.

'There's a patch of anhydrosis around the bite,' I told him.

'What's that?' he demanded.

'No sweating,' I said. I confess I had deliberately used the medical term because I was fed up with being treated like a half-witted criminal. 'That rather suggests that you were bitten by a false black widow spider.'

'Good God!' said the woman I assumed to be Lady something or other. 'A black widow spider? Do you mean to say that there are black widow spiders in Devon?'

'Not a black widow,' I said. 'There are spiders called false black widows. I think there are quite a lot of varieties. Over a hundred, I believe. This was probably one of those. I've seen one or two. They're said to have come over from Madeira in a bunch of bananas back in the 19th century and they've been here ever since. I don't think they usually bite but if it was tucked away comfortably in Sir Felix's boot and then a foot suddenly appeared it probably felt rather threatened.'

'I bet it did!' said Sir Felix. 'And it had good reason to feel threatened. I squashed it. The damned little thing had the audacity to bite me!'

'Most people in North Devon cover up their boots and shoes, especially if they leave them in a garage or an outhouse,' I said. 'An old tin lid will do fine to keep the spiders out.'

'Should Sir Felix go to hospital?' asked the woman. She frowned as something awful occurred to her. 'Is there a hospital around here?' she asked.

'A hospital isn't necessary,' I said. 'The symptoms will die down in a day or two.'

'What about treatment?'

'We'll just wash the area and put on some antiseptic cream,' I said. 'And I'll give you some antihistamine tablets to take away the discomfort.'

'My valet has already washed it,' said Sir Felix.

'Fine,' I said, 'then I'll just put on a little antiseptic cream.'

I cleaned the skin around the bite with some antiseptic wipes and then put on a little antiseptic cream. I found some antihistamine tablets in my bag and put them on his bedside table. I wasn't surprised when he didn't thank me. These were not thanking people.

'I've found the pyjamas ma'am,' said the woman in black, holding up several pairs of expensive looking striped pyjamas. She sounded relieved, as though she might have expected to have been beaten if she hadn't managed to find them.

I helped Sir Felix remove his sodden pyjamas and replace them with a new pair. I told him that I'd visit again the following day. And then I headed for the door and back downstairs. No one said thank you. I wondered if anyone might offer to give me a lift back home but no one did. Nor did anyone offer to lend me a pair of shoes or boots. The slightly mysterious, and massively superior, lady of the house, who had stayed behind for a moment at the behest of Sir Felix, followed in my footsteps down the stairs.

'Sir Felix said to give him two pounds,' she said to the butler when we reached the hallway downstairs. The butler, still dressed immaculately, had appeared as if from nowhere.

The butler removed a wallet from his inside pocket and removed two brand new one pound notes. They looked as if they had been ironed. He held them out to me. I held up a hand. 'No thank you,' I said. The butler who seemed shocked looked to his mistress for advice.

'Sir Felix was treated as an NHS patient,' I told him. 'I'll bring a form with me tomorrow.'

The lady of the house seemed startled by this. But before she could speak, I opened the front door and walked back out into the night. It was still raining and it was still windy but I was glad to be out of there.

When I got back to Bilbury Grange it was dawn and I was freezing cold, weary and footsore. I checked that no more calls had come in and then I washed, shaved and dressed in dry, warm clothes. I then made myself breakfast. Fresh grapefruit, egg on toast and four slices of toast with marmalade. Patsy was still asleep. When I'd eaten my fill, and drunk two cups of coffee, I telephoned Tolstoys, the local garage, and asked one of the mechanics to retrieve the Rolls Royce. I told him where he could find it.

The mechanic knocked on the door 30 minutes later.

'Have you mended her already?' I said, delighted.

'Wonderful car, doctor,' said the mechanic.

'It is,' I agreed proudly.

'But marvellous as it is,' he said gently, 'I'm afraid that it still needs regular doses of petrol in order to function at its best.'

He explained that the Rolls had shuddered to a halt because it had run out of petrol.

'The spare two gallon container that you had in the boot was enough to get it moving again,' he said.

I made him promise not to tell a soul.

When I turned up at The Castle later that day, I tooted the horn to announce my arrival. And when the butler opened the front door and saw the Rolls Royce standing there, he actually called me 'sir'. I had a feeling that there was a slight forward inclination of the body, too. Not quite a bow, you understand, but a movement heading in that general direction.

I still thought that the wretched fellow might have done the decent thing and found me a towel the previous evening.

Sir Felix was a good deal better, though still as snotty and as bad tempered.

And two days later he had made a complete physical recovery.

Mentally and spiritually he was quite beyond my help.

I never did find out who he was or the nature of his relationship with the woman who had told the butler to offer me two pounds for my services.

I asked Frank, who tends to know everyone in North Devon, even if they're just passing through the county on their way from or to somewhere else, and he said he thought Sir Felix was a millionaire who had made his money out of property development and running a chain of shops. Frank said he had heard that Sir Felix had allegedly been given his knighthood for 'public services', but everyone knew he had bought it, having made several large donations to one of the large political parties. Moreover, the money he had given had not been his own but belonged to the companies of which he was a director. According to Frank, a number of angry shareholders felt that the knighthood was theirs as much as his and one aggrieved pensioner had made this point at a rather heated Annual General Meeting.

Frank also said that Sir Felix had a number of honorary degrees which he had purchased from British universities. I didn't know this but Frank assured me that if you gave a few quid to a university, they would reward you with an honorary degree of your choice.

Frank said he thought that Sir Felix and his mistress lived in Monaco and came to the mansion in East Morton for no more than one week a year. He said they brought their own servants with them from Monaco and left the house shut up when they weren't using it.

The world we live in never fails to surprise me.

As a country GP, I see people living in grand houses and I see people living in tiny two room cottages.

In my experience, the people in the grand houses are, on the whole, likely to be self-obsessed, mean and thoughtless while the people in the tiny cottages are far more likely to be thoughtful, kind and generous.

No small cottage owner would have let me walk out into the rain without insisting that I borrow a coat or an umbrella or both. If they'd had a car or a cart, they would have insisted on taking me back home.

Life's funny like that.

The Austrian Émigré in Smithy-on-the-Moor

When I was 18-years-old, I spent a year working in a part of Liverpool called Kirkby as a Community Service Volunteer. A man called Alec Dickson, the charismatic founder of the organisation, had persuaded me to give a year of my life to help a community where people were struggling to survive. It sounds terribly twee but it wasn't. My parents had worked and saved hard and, as a result, I had spent my formative years in a comfortably middle class environment. My waking hours had been dedicated to the acquisition of the certificates required to make the next move up the academic ladder. I had finished school and had acquired the pieces of paper necessary to go to university to start my medical studies but I was tired of textbooks and examinations and I wanted to spend a year in the real world before I plunged myself into another five or six years of academic life.

Alec Dickson made duty and responsibility sound necessary and invigorating and inspired me to give the time to do something to help in a community which was, to say the least, troubled.

The local buses always had a police car escorting them and the windows of all the shops and public buildings (including the police station) were protected by thick steel mesh.

Violence was a way of life and the area was controlled by a series of gangs. Just the place for an 18-year-old who arrived wearing an old school blazer partly because he didn't know any better, partly because he didn't have anything else to wear and partly because there was a lot of wear left in it.

I did many things in Liverpool (including form an army of young volunteers prepared to give their evenings and weekends to improve the lives of their elderly neighbours by decorating, gardening and shopping) but one of my more mundane responsibilities was to drive a Meals on Wheels van.

Once a twice a week, I would climb behind the wheel of a clapped out old vehicle (which would have never passed a road test if they'd been invented then), roll it down an incline in order to get it going and drive around Kirkby delivering hot meals to the elderly, the frail and the sick; people who had been pretty much abandoned by society in general and the welfare state in particular.

Everyone who received those meals welcomed them with open arms and big smiles and I had absolutely no doubt that a good many of the recipients did not eat hot food on the days when the Meals on Wheels van didn't arrive.

The Meals on Wheels service in Bilbury was organised and run by Patsy (my wife), Mrs Kennet (Patsy's mother), Adrienne (Patsy's sister), Anne Robinson aka Thwaites (Thumper Robinson's partner in life) and a dozen other locals.

The fact that the meals were cooked and delivered by women was not something that was done by choice or some sort of sexist division of labour. It just happened that way and in the 1970s, it was not considered strange in any way.

The meals were provided free of charge and the delivery drivers used their own vehicles and provided their own petrol. The women running the service took turns to prepare the meals (all of which were made from fresh, home grown ingredients which were served in very generous portions) and they had a more than adequate collection of metal serving dishes, complete with covers, which had been acquired by Patchy Fogg when a hotel in Taunton had closed its doors and there had been a sale of furniture, crockery and kitchen equipment.

It had once been suggested that the women might apply to the local council for a grant to help defray their costs but they had unanimously rejected the suggestion on the grounds that once the council got involved, men with clipboards would be following them around checking to see how much gravy was poured onto Mrs Fretwell's potatoes and how many sprouts had been put onto Mr Barton's plate.

At Christmas, at Easter and on their birthdays, the recipients of these meals each received a half bottle of wine, and these extras were paid for by an annual summer fete and bring-and-buy sale and an equally annual winter jumble sale.

No one thought any of this was exceptional and neither donors nor recipients regarded the Meals on Wheels service as demeaning or patronising in any way.

A visitor from London, who found out about the service, said that it was a very Victorian thing to do, that it smacked of soup kitchens and that such services should be provided by the State.

However, no one in Bilbury could quite understand why food handed out by the State would be any more satisfying than food handed out by warm-hearted, generous individuals who did what they did because they wanted to rather than because they had to.

One of the advantages of having such a service in the village was that the women delivering the meals could keep an eye on villagers who were elderly, frail or vulnerable in some way. And they could, of course, pass any concerns on to me.

'My Mum saw a man called Axel Heidberg today,' said Patsy, one evening. 'We only put him onto our rota for meals this week. I don't know where she got his name from but she said that he cried when she delivered his meal. She had a look in his kitchen and said it looked as though he'd been living on a diet of dry, stale cornflakes and packet soup. We're going to deliver meals to him every day. And Mum took him a bag of groceries, tea, bread, milk, sugar and so on, which she bought from Peter Marshall. Peter also gave her half a dozen badly dented tins of fruit and soup – the ones that he usually sells at a discount.'

'Peter gave her some tins? Gave her as in 'without charging for them'?'

'Yes!'

'Peter Marshall? The man who once tried to charge me double for a packet of biscuits because he said they were so old that they could be classified as antiques and were an investment?'

'He didn't!'

'He darned well did!'

'Yes, but he can be generous sometimes.'

'So it seems,' I said, unable to hide my surprise at discovering this hidden side to Peter Marshall.

'And my Mum can be very charming when she wants to be.'

'Indeed, she can.'

'Anyway, Mum wonders if you'd pop in and see him. Just give him a bit of a check-up.'

I took the address and promised to visit him the following day. Neither the name nor the address was familiar.

And, the next day, to my quiet astonishment, I discovered why: I had never met Mr Heidberg before and Dr Brownlow had never met him either.

Mr Heidberg, who had been born in Austria, had been living in the village for half a century and was living like a hermit. He had quite slipped through the cracks of the State's welfare programme.

I had no idea how Mrs Kennet had found him. He lived on the outskirts of a hamlet called Smithy-on-the-Moor, which is four or five miles away, on the Barnstaple side of Bilbury.

I have always been fascinated by how villages develop and acquire their names.

Villages and towns sometimes develop in one particular spot through convenience. So, for example, London originally became a settlement because a gravel bottom to the river meant that it was the best place to cross the Thames. Spots which are sheltered or easily defended were popular sites for a small development in the Middle Ages. In England, it is common for a village to develop around a farm which opened a public house in a room or outbuilding. (It used to be very easy to open a pub in England. All you needed was a room, something alcoholic to sell to customers and a barmaid or barman to serve the stuff.)

Some villages get their name from a prominent landowner or from a topographical oddity.

Lynmouth, a little way to the east along the coast from Combe Martin, got its name because the word 'lyn' means torrent. Those who named the village got it right; on the 15th of August in 1952, ten inches of rain fell on Exmoor in 24 hours, two branches of the river flooded down steep sided narrow valleys, gathering boulders and destroying cottages in Lynmouth. The river drowned 34 people that night. History books show that similar things happened in 1607 and 1770. It is clear that the Saxons, who named the river, knew what they were doing.

Ilfracombe, the largest tourist resort in North Devon, is the valley belonging to someone called Alfred, though just who Alfred was is a mystery now. It almost certainly wasn't Alfred the Great, the monarch renowned for his cake burning escapade.

Other villages acquire their name because there is a shop or business of some kind in the locality.

And so I have no doubt that Smithy-on-the-Moor was, as the name makes it clear, named because there used to be a blacksmith on the site and the site is on Exmoor.

There certainly isn't a blacksmith there now and the hamlet is so small that it's not surprising that its name no longer appears on modern local maps.

If the keeper of the local electoral roll ever did a census, they would probably find that there was only one name to put on the register under the name Smithy-on-the-Moor. And that name would be Axel Heidberg.

It wasn't easy to find Mr Heidberg's tiny, run down cottage.

Following the instructions given to me by Mrs Kennet, I took a small, pretty well unused track between two fields and eventually had to give up, stop the car and walk the rest of the way on foot. The track was rough and narrow and so uneven that I could hear the bottom of the Rolls scraping along on bits of rock and stone. Mrs Kennet drives her husband's elderly Land Rover, which is built for such rough terrain.

Mr Heidberg, when I finally reached his home, told me that he wasn't quite sure how old he was but that he was pretty sure that he had been born in February in Austria and that in England, Queen Victoria had been on the throne at the time.

He told me that his father had been a doctor who had worked in Germany and that the family had moved to England at some point shortly after the end of the First World War. He couldn't remember precisely why the family had emigrated but said that although he was, by that time, living alone in an apartment in a building in Heidelberg he had accompanied his parents to England because they were both rather elderly and frail.

His father had been in his sixties when Mr Heidberg was born and his mother was what doctors tend to refer to as a 'mature' mother.

The family's modest fortune, which had been invested in German banks, took a steep dive when the German Mark was destroyed by the dramatic rates of inflation which characterised the early 1920s.

A small amount of money had been raised by the sale of Mrs Heidberg's jewellery but she and her husband died within a few years of each other and the house they had been renting, and which Mr Heidberg had been sharing with them, was repossessed when there was no money left to pay the rent.

'I miss them still,' said Mr Heidberg. 'They were both quite old when they died and I remember there were some who dismissed their deaths with the cruel comment that they had both enjoyed 'a good innings'. But I did not understand that attitude. It is, perhaps, a peculiarly English way of looking at things. Dying when we are old is no less a tragedy than dying when we are young. We feel sadness for the young who die unfulfilled, their lives just starting, but we may miss the elderly just as much if not more for we have known them for longer and we miss their wisdom, their experience, their knowledge.'

Mr Heidberg had sold the small amount of furniture which remained and had kept only an old accordion which had belonged to his father and which he had, as a boy, taught himself to play. He had toured England's coast giving performances on beaches and at hotels. When the accordion was damaged by vandals who disliked his German accent, he had become a 'gentleman of the road', sleeping rough and doing odd jobs at farms to earn enough money to buy a little food.

And he had ended up in Smithy-on-the-Moor, where, after sleeping under hedges and in barns for a fortnight, he had discovered the empty, derelict cottage he had adopted as his own.

No one had ever tried to throw him out but he still lived in constant fear that one day the owner would turn up and he would be evicted.

I don't think he could quite believe me when I told him that according to English law the cottage now belonged to him and nobody could throw him out.

I gave Mr Heidberg as good a check-up as I could. I couldn't weigh him because I didn't have any scales with me and he certainly didn't have any but he was clearly not overweight. I couldn't test blood or urine samples (I didn't have any blood or urine specimen bottles with me) but I checked his heart, his lungs and his blood pressure and I gave his nervous system a fairly comprehensive test.

I couldn't do a proper eye test but I looked at his fundi with my ophthalmoscope and checked his visual acuity by scribbling some letters on an old piece of cardboard. My informal examination showed no abnormalities. His joints all seemed to be in excellent condition too.

'You're pretty fit for whatever your age is,' I told him when I'd finished.

'You don't have to be ill just because you are old,' said Mr Heidberg wisely.

'Indeed not,' I agreed.

Looking around, it was clear that although Mr Heidberg himself was in pretty good condition, the same could not be said for his home which was, to say the least, rather primitive. There was no electricity and no gas, of course, and the only water supply came from a spring in the garden. Long, long ago someone had connected a piece of lead piping to a collecting funnel in the spring in order to feed a tap in the kitchen. The pipe had developed a leak and there was a bowl underneath the pipe to catch the water which dripped from it constantly. A privy which sat over a cesspit completed the amenities.

The house was packed with bits and pieces of furniture and crockery, most of which looked as if it had probably been salvaged from a rubbish heap. There were five wooden dining chairs in the living room but four of them were so badly broken that they were useless except as fuel. Indeed that was probably why Mr Heidberg had them there for the only heating in the house came, as was so common in Bilbury homes, from an open fireplace.

Water had come in through a hole in the roof and had damaged the ceiling in the downstairs living room and one of the downstairs sash windows had jammed open with the result that an icy cold draught swept through all the downstairs rooms. I could not begin to imagine how cold the house must have been in the winter. 'When there is snow outside then I also have snow in my living room,' said Mr Heidberg.

I pushed and pulled at the window and eventually managed to move it. Once it was freed, I could close it.

I then went upstairs with him into one of the bedrooms.

The hole in the roof, which had caused all the damage inside the house, was about two feet square and I guessed that at least half a dozen slates must have come loose and disappeared off the roof and into the overgrown garden beneath.

'The first thing to do is to mend the roof,' I told him.

'I agree,' said Mr Heidberg. 'I tried to climb up there myself but I have no ladder and when I tried to climb onto a water butt by the back door, I fell onto the ground and hurt my arm.' He showed me a healing bruise on his forearm. I told him that he had been lucky not to break anything and he agreed with this assessment.

I was, as I have so often been, quietly astonished at the way people will survive in adverse circumstances. The young believe they are immortal and they have not, in any case, been around long enough to have acquired a real and lasting affection for life; but it is the elderly, who know only too well that they are mortal, and who have seen the consequences of mortality, cling to life with the ferocity of a bargain hunter who has taken hold of her prey in a department store sale.

Suddenly, looking up at the hole in the roof, I had a brainwave.

'Do you have an umbrella?' I asked him.

Mr Heidberg went downstairs and rummaged around in the cupboard under the stairs. A couple of minutes later he re-joined me; this time he was clutching a large, colourful golf umbrella which advertised a well-known Scottish bank.

I took the umbrella from him, climbed onto a stout and rather ugly looking chest of drawers and then stuffed the umbrella up through the hole in the roof. Once the umbrella was through the hole, I put it up and then pulled down on the handle so that the umbrella sat on the roof, covering up the hole very effectively.

'But won't it blow away when there is wind?' asked Mr Heidberg.

'It would,' I agreed. 'But it isn't going to if you've got some stout string somewhere.'

Mr Heidberg went back downstairs, revisited the cupboard under the stairs and returned clutching a ball of blue baler twine. Most things in Bilbury are held together with baler twine and as far as I am aware, there are only two colours available: blue or orange. I then used several lengths of baler twine to tie the handle of the umbrella to the handles on the stout and ugly chest of drawers.

Mr Heidberg was delighted.

'I don't know how long it will last,' I warned him. 'But I'll try to find someone who can come and put on some new slates for you.

'Why do you all do these kind things for me?' he asked. There were tears rolling down both cheeks.

'In Bilbury, we like to help each other out,' I explained. 'I'm just so sorry that we didn't know you were here. But now that we have found you, we won't forget you.'

'Kind and beautiful ladies now bring me food,' said Mr Heidberg. 'Hot food, every day!'

'I know,' I said. 'One of the beautiful ladies is my wife, Patsy. Another is her mother. And a third is my wife's sister.'

'But I have no money!' said Mr Heidberg. 'I cannot pay them.'

'They don't expect you to,' I assured him.

He seemed overcome with what was happening and opened his mouth but did not say anything.

'I'll try to find someone to come and mend your roof,' I told him.

'No, no!' said Mr Heidberg, shaking his head. 'That is too much. It is all too much. I cannot accept all these kindnesses. I have no money.'

I thought for a moment and then looked around. 'Maybe there is something in your house which is of value,' I suggested. 'Would you like me to ask a friend of mine to come and take a look? Maybe there is an old chair or piece of pottery that would raise some money for you.' I knew that a proud old man like Mr Heidberg would feel better if he thought that he was paying his way.

'That, I would like very much!' said Mr Heidberg.

We shook hands, and I promised to return in a day or two's time with a friend who would, hopefully, be able to find something which could be turned into cash.

And so, two days later, I returned to Smithy-on-the-Moor with Patchy Fogg, my good friend, my brother-in-law and the best antique dealer in Devon.

Patchy was still flush with cash after having identified and sold a marble-topped table at a house auction sale. He had made a small fortune from the sale of the table which the auctioneer and every other dealer had completely missed. The table had been sitting in a conservatory, in plain view, but it had been covered with pot plants. Since then he has, on several occasions, shown himself to be enormously generous to needy Bilburians by purchasing small items for rather more than their true value.

'The doctor says you'd like me to see if there's anything in the house worth a little money,' said Patchy.

'I would like that very much,' said the old man.

'Is there anything here of sentimental value?' asked Patchy. 'Anything that you wouldn't want to part with?'

'Nothing,' said Mr Heidberg.

And so Patchy took a look around. Mr Heidberg and I watched him anxiously.

'Aha!' said Patchy eventually, spotting the bowl which was being used to catch the leaks from the lead pipe which brought water in from the spring outside in the garden. He picked up the bowl, replaced it with an old saucepan he took off a shelf, and examined it carefully.

'Would you sell this bowl?' Patchy asked.

'You can have it,' replied Mr Heidberg.

'No, no,' said Patchy. 'I would like to buy it. Would you sell it to me?'

'If you think it is worth anything I would very happily sell it,' said Mr Heidberg. 'It is only an old bowl.'

'I think it might fetch £100 at auction,' said Patchy. 'How about I give you £90 for it?'

'That is too much,' replied Mr Heidberg. 'If it is worth £100 at auction then you should pay me no more than £50. That is very fair.'

They settled on £75.

Mr Heidberg thought that too generous but Patchy insisted that he would not give any less. He counted out the notes and handed them to Mr Heidberg.

We got into the Rolls to leave and Patchy tossed the bowl into the back of the car.

'Crumbs!' I said. 'Do you always treat valuable bits of porcelain in such a debonair fashion?'

'It's not valuable and it's not porcelain,' laughed Patchy.

I started the car and we drove away. 'How much is it really worth?' I asked him.

'It's not worth tuppence,' said Patchy. 'It was made for Woolworths and sold there by the lorry load in the 1950s.'

'You're an old softy!' I told him.

'That's what my wife says,' replied Patchy.

A fortnight later, I returned to Smithy-on-the-Moor to check on Mr Heidberg. He was looking good. His roof had been repaired and he was still getting his hot meals every day. The leak in the pipe in his kitchen had been repaired too.

'I have found another of those bowls,' he said, as I was about to leave.

'Which bowls?' I asked, having forgotten.

'The same as the one your friend liked so much,' said Mr Heidberg. There was a sparkle of hope in his eyes. 'Do you think he would like to buy another?'

'I'll have a word with him,' I said, hoping that Patchy was still feeling flush and generous.

He was.

Three months later, Patchy had three worthless bowls and his wallet was £225 lighter.

'I hope that old man of yours hasn't got too many more of those damned bowls,' said Patchy, after he'd paid for the third one.

Mrs Leeson's Leg

Margaret Leeson and her husband Henry live in a splendid old manor house that is hidden away behind the highest yew hedge I have ever seen.

The house has been in Mrs Leeson's family for generations and her father served as a Minister in Winston Churchill's war time cabinet.

Henry Leeson was described to me as being 'something in the City of London' and when I asked what this meant I was told that it meant that he sat on the boards of half a dozen large, well-established companies where his job was to nod, munch biscuits and say 'harrumph' occasionally whenever anything unconventional was proposed.

I thought this sounded rather oppressive until I realised that there was probably some commercial value in having someone on the board of directors who questioned change in case it was being proposed for the sake of it, rather than to improve the company's prospects and profits.

The Leesons could, I suppose, have been described as eccentric in some of their ways, though they certainly wouldn't have said that there was anything remotely eccentric about any aspect of their lives. Indeed, they would have doubtless been affronted if they had ever heard the word 'eccentric' used to describe them.

Both well into their seventies but perfect examples of both agerasia and ataraxia, they saw themselves as stalwarts of the English countryside, solid patriots of the Old English variety; unbending, unchanging and reliable in their honest affection for tradition and traditional values. Today, they would be dismissed as feudal, anachronistic and embarrassingly out of their time, but back in the 1970s they were widely respected and admired for their determination to stick to standards which had long been regarded as having little or no relevance.

They dressed every evening for dinner.

He wore a dinner jacket with a bow tie and cummerbund. The bow tie was, of course, self-tied. He would have no more dreamt of wearing a ready-made bow tie on a piece of elastic than he would have dreamt of wearing a red cummerbund or a pair of gold hoop earrings in pirate style.

She always wore a posh frock and jewellery which other women might have kept in a bank vault.

They had a butler called Cecil, a housekeeper called Mary, a valet called George, a lady's maid called Jane, a cook called Edith, two kitchen staff both called Perkins and three gardeners all called Jim. They also had a groom/chauffeur who was called Wallace.

When I expressed some puzzlement about their ability to find gardeners all with the same name, Mr Leeson told me that they always called their servants by the same names. So, their butlers were always called Cecil, their housekeepers were always called Mary and, so on and so on. All their gardeners were always called Jim. Mr Leeson did not seem to think that there was anything unusual, exceptional or demeaning in this curious domestic ritual and the staff didn't seem to mind either. 'It makes it easy to remember their names,' explained Mr Leeson, when I asked him why they did this. 'And it avoids the potential embarrassment of getting a name wrong.'

At Christmas time, the Leesons held a carol service in their hall (which was big enough to fit the average sized cottage with room to spare for a garage and a garden shed) and in June every year, they held a fete in their garden in aid of the local church. (Bilbury has a good many summer fetes, all well attended.)

Mrs Leeson travelled around the village in a tilbury gig, pulled by a splendidly active grey mare which had a high stepping gait and a turn of speed which would, I suspect, have worried many a race horse. The horse pulling the gig was always called Gigi which seemed unusually appropriate.

Whenever I heard Mrs Leeson's gig approaching along one of the Bilbury lanes (and you could hear the clip clop of the horse some distance away), I would pull into the nearest gateway and wait for her to pass.

I saw them as patients only occasionally for they were, on the whole, an exceptionally healthy couple.

But early one evening I received a telephone call from Cecil the butler who, after apologising for the call and what he described as 'the inevitable inconvenience', then asked if I would be kind enough to visit Mrs Leeson as soon as might be convenient. Cecil was himself well past the customary retiring age and age had given him all the dignity and aloofness of a butler appearing in a story by P.G.Wodehouse. He had a way of talking that was all his own. I could not imagine him ever panicking or finding himself in a situation which he could not manage without breaking a sweat.

'Would she like me to visit in the morning or this evening?' I asked.

'Mrs Leeson would probably say that she would be happy to see you tomorrow morning but, to be honest with you, sir, and I hope you don't mind my mentioning it, I have talked briefly to Jane, Mrs Leeson's personal maid, who is, of course, more au fait with Mrs Leeson's present condition, than myself and we both feel that this evening would be preferable, sir,' replied Cecil.

I told him that I would leave straight away and should be knocking on the door within fifteen minutes at the very most.

Cecil said that that would be both most agreeable and much appreciated.

'I'm so sorry that Cecil bothered you,' said Mrs Leeson, who was lying in a four poster bed, propped up on four or five pillows. She was wearing a peach coloured nightdress and had a thin shawl around her shoulders. She was having difficulty in breathing and her skin was red and clearly flushed. A woman of about 30 or 35, whom I did not recognise, was standing on one side of the bed. Henry Leeson was standing at the other side of the bed. Both looked very concerned. The young woman was wearing what I took to be the standard, traditional uniform of a maid and I assumed that she was Jane, Mrs Leeson's personal maid.

I asked Mrs Leeson what had happened.

'I really don't know, doctor,' she replied. She spoke with some difficulty because her breathing rate was fast and she was clearly short of breath. It was an effort for her to produce each word. She seemed rather slow, even confused. She had to look at me for quite a while before finally recognising me.

I put the back of my hand on her forehead, which was red. She was very hot. Her skin was mottled. I checked her pulse. It was racing.

'Actually, I feel rather awful, doctor,' she said. 'I feel as though I am about to die. Do you think I'm about to die, doctor?' Her speech seemed slurred.

'You appear to have an infection,' I told her. 'But there's absolutely no reason to believe that you're going to die.'

At this point, I really didn't have the faintest idea how ill she really was. But there was clearly no point in making things worse by making her worry. I firmly believe that a doctor should, whenever possible and appropriate, try to reassure and comfort his patients. The curative powers of a reassuring, confident doctor have been shown to be just as good as those of quite significantly large doses of the most powerful medication.

'How long have you been feeling poorly,' I asked her.

'Most of the day,' she replied. 'Actually, I was rather poorly yesterday. So I suppose it started yesterday.'

'We thought it was just a bit of a bug, at first,' added her husband. I guessed he probably wanted to help his wife avoid having to answer too many questions. 'She's been going hot and cold.'

'Has she vomited at all?'

'Twice.' Mr Leeson looked across at the maid who nodded.

'Any bowel problems? Diarrhoea for example?'

'No.' This time it was the maid who spoke.

I rolled up the sleeve of Mrs Leeson's nightdress and took her blood pressure. It was low.

'Do you have any pains?' I asked her.

'Everywhere,' she replied. 'My legs and my arms and my back.' She paused to take a deep breath. 'I have pains everywhere.'

'She's been shivery and at one point she felt quite cold,' said Mr Leeson.

'And Mrs Leeson has been sweating quite a lot,' added the maid.

'Glowing, dear,' corrected Mrs Leeson. 'Only horses sweat.'

'I'm sorry, ma'am,' said the maid. But she smiled. 'Horses sweat, men perspire and ladies glow.'

'Exactly,' said Mrs Leeson.

'Have you had any tingling in your hands?'

Mrs Leeson thought for a while. 'No,' said. 'No, I don't think so.'

'Any tingling in your feet?'

'No, I haven't.'

'That's good,' I said.

I was pretty sure that Mrs Leeson had sepsis – a rather serious, sometimes deadly, condition in which the body reacts badly to an infection of some kind. The whole body sometimes overreacts and shuts down, sometimes reducing the blood flow to vital organs. It is, indeed, a real emergency which needs to be taken very seriously. I was glad to hear that neither her hands nor her feet were tingling because when that happens it rather suggests that they are being starved of oxygen and that the muscles and the skin are starting to die. It's not a good sign.

Many different types of infection can trigger a reaction of this type. A chest infection or a urinary infection can sometimes result in one of these nasty shock reactions.

'Have you had any sort of chest infection?' I asked Mrs Leeson.

She shook her head.

'Any urinary infection?'

She thought for a moment, as though the question were a difficult one. 'No, I don't think so,' she said. She turned towards her maid. 'Have I?'

'No, ma'am,' replied the maid, who clearly knew her mistress very well.

'You haven't had to go to hospital at all recently? Even as a visitor?'

'No,' she replied. 'I haven't been away from Bilbury for more than a month. I've been busy helping in the garden.'

'My wife likes to help prepare some of our flowers, fruits and vegetables for the village show,' explained Mr Leeson.

'Have you cut yourself at all? Scratched yourself?'

'I don't think so,' replied Mrs Leeson. She turned to her husband. 'Have I dear?'

'Not that I know of,' replied her husband.

'Actually,' said the maid, speaking softly and clearly rather embarrassed at contradicting both of her employers at the same time, 'if you don't mind my saying so, ma'am, you did scratch your leg on the rose bushes. You had a nasty scratch about two inches long. It bled a little. I had to throw away your stocking.'

'I didn't know that,' said Mr Leeson.

'It was a very small scratch, sir,' said the maid, who now seemed rather apologetic about mentioning it.

'Can I see the scratch?' I asked.

'I'll just pop outside,' said Mr Leeson, speaking softly and tip toeing towards the door. 'Call me when you're finished.'

I watched him go with some surprise.

The maid pulled back the bedclothes so that I could see Mrs Leeson's leg. There was a nasty looking scratch on the back of her left calf.

'Do you think that could have anything to do with it?' she asked.

'I think that is the cause of it,' I replied firmly. I quickly checked to make sure that there were no signs or symptoms of tetanus or lockjaw – jaw muscles in spasm, difficulty in swallowing, muscle stiffness and spasms elsewhere. There weren't.

'Do you think Mrs Leeson will need to go to hospital?' asked the maid when she had replaced the bed clothes. She then went to the door to tell Mr Leeson he could come back into his wife's bedroom.

'I'd rather treat her here,' I said. 'It's a long way to travel in an ambulance. And I'm afraid hospitals are full of infections.'

'What sort of treatment?' asked Mr Leeson.

'Antibiotics,' I said firmly. 'I'm going to start Mrs Leeson on a strong antibiotic straight away.' I took a packet of antibiotics out of my black medical bag and handed them to Mr Leeson. I told him how they had to be administered.

'You must call me if there is any new symptom or any change, particularly any deterioration,' I told him and the maid. 'Don't wait – call me immediately. If I need to visit I can be here within 15 minutes.'

They promised they would do so.

When I visited after the surgery the next morning, I was massively relieved to see that Mrs Leeson was slightly better. She wasn't completely restored to health, but she was looking and feeling better than she had been the night before. The antibiotics had clearly started to do their work.

It took nearly a week for her to make a recovery.

At the time, I remember being grateful that we were able to use good antibiotics to tackle such infections.

What I feared at the time, and wrote about in numerous articles and medical books, was that the overuse of antibiotics (both by doctors and by farmers) would result in many bugs acquiring resistance.

These days, many patients who have acquired sepsis as a result of an infection die because antibiotics no longer work.

But, that is now and this was then.

Mrs Leeson made a complete recovery and was able to see several items from her garden win prizes at the Bilbury Village Show.

Ironically, the roses which had nearly killed her only managed third place.

The Bicyclists

Thumper had been to the hairdresser.

'Anne has been nagging me for months to get it cut,' he said. 'She said I looked disreputable.'

'You are disreputable,' Patchy pointed out with unarguable honesty.

'You look younger,' I told Thumper.

He ignored Patchy and glowered at me. 'That's what Anne said. I don't want to look younger. I want to look older.' He grinned. 'I was hoping to look old enough to be able to get into the cinema to see the saucy movies.'

'You could always find an adult to go with you,' I suggested.

'I don't know any adults,' responded Thumper quickly.

There was no sensible answer to that so nobody said anything.

We were sitting in the snug in the Duck and Puddle.

Thumper had his usual medicine, a pint of Old Restoration; a brew so toxic that it burns permanent marks if spilt onto a wooden table top. Patchy was drinking a glass of very dry white wine. I had a glass of Glenfarclas, one of my top ten favourite of all the Scottish malts. Frank, who had drunk his daily allowance of alcohol, was sipping a ginger beer, a beverage for which he has recently professed a great and surprising liking.

'Adrienne was watching television when I got home yesterday evening,' said Patchy, obviously triggered by Thumper's reference to the cinema. 'She was watching some programme about hospitals. They were showing an operation.' Patchy shuddered. 'Awful.' He shuddered again. 'Adrienne had prepared a mixed grill for dinner. Sausages with a nice piece of liver, a couple of kidneys and some fried onions. I don't know how she can watch these programmes. It nearly put me off my food.' He shuddered again.

'They have these medical programmes on the television all the time,' said Thumper. 'Anne was watching a programme about childbirth the other day. This Irish woman called Murphy was having triplets. Who could possibly be interested in that?'

'Mr Murphy?' I said.

'We should all be grateful for small Murphys,' muttered Patchy.

I looked at him and raised an eyebrow in acknowledgement and appreciation.

Patchy smiled modestly.

One of these days they'll have a channel devoted to this sort of thing,' said Thumper deliberately ignoring Patchy's bon mot. 'They'll set up a camera in an operating theatre and just show whatever is happening – 24 hour operating theatre.'

'A lot of the time there isn't anything much happening,' I pointed out. 'Except for someone scrubbing the walls and floor.'

'People would watch that,' said Thumper without hesitation. 'It would be better than that potter's wheel they show.'

'Do they still show that?' asked Patchy.

Suddenly the door burst open and the peace of the early afternoon was shattered by two youths who came into the snug as though they were being chased by wild dogs. They looked to be in their early 20s. One was tall and the other was not. The tall one had shoulder length hair tied back in a ponytail. The short one, who seemed to have had his mouth sewn into a scowl, had one of those standard short-back-and-sides haircuts which customers got in the 1960s when they forget to tell the barber how they wanted him to cut their hair. It was a hairstyle popular with schoolteachers and parents. The two newcomers were both wearing khaki shorts and open-necked, short-sleeved shirts.

'Shop!' shouted the tall one in that rude way some impatient people shout when they walk into a shop, find it temporarily empty, and want to be served.

The short one laughed a good deal as though this were the funniest thing he'd ever heard. It may well have been. He was young and looked as if his experience of life was probably limited to the twin excitements of getting up in the morning and going to bed at night.

'We've cycled from Barnstaple,' said the tall one, answering a question no one had asked and giving an answer which was, I fear, of little interest to anyone present.

I looked out of the window and there were two racing bicycles leaning against a wall outside the pub.

I looked to check because I was once in the Duck and Puddle with Frank and Thumper when two Austrians turned up. One, a male, looked to be in his 40s. He had grey hair and a grey beard and wore a tweed jacket, which had a little belt at the back, and a pair of bottle green corduroy trousers. His companion, a woman, looked to be slightly older. She had red hair which stretched down to her waist and she wore what we later discovered was traditional Austrian costume: a dirndl and a white blouse.

They each ordered a glass of red wine, and a dish of Gilly's famous hotpot, though they probably didn't know at the time that it was famous.

We all chatted a little and Thumper asked them what they were doing in Devon. They said, or we thought they said, that they were cyclists and that they had been attending a festival in Glastonbury. They were now taking a few days holiday. Neither of them looked as if they were cyclists, and they certainly weren't dressed for cycling, but appearances can be deceptive and, as Thumper pointed out afterwards, they were Continental Europeans and you can never tell with people who come from the other side of the Channel. After all, it is a place where men wear leather shorts and slap their thighs at the drop of a hat.

It was summer at the time so it was raining heavily.

'Do you want to put your machines under cover?' asked Frank, who has a more generous heart than is sometimes appreciated.

The Austrians looked at him, puzzled. (We didn't know then that they were Austrian, although we knew that they were certainly foreign.)

'Your bikes,' said Frank. 'Do you want to put your bicycles in my shed?'

'Bicycles?' said the man, frowning and looking puzzled. 'What is it with the bicycles?'

'You said that you were cyclists,' Frank pointed out.

'Not at all,' said the man, now even more puzzled. 'I have a bicycle never ridden. Not once in my life have I a bicycle ridden.' He turned to his companion and spoke to her in what I now assume must have been German. She, looking quite indignant, shook her head.

It turned out that they were both psychics, which explained, I suppose, why they had been to Glastonbury. There's a lot of that sort of thing going on there.

Once everything had been sorted out, they were friendly enough in a cold, distant and rather superior sort of way. Frank, Thumper and I laughed about it. We thought it was quite a funny mistake. But the two foreigners, being Austrian and therefore not having an English sense of humour, didn't laugh at all, of course. And they didn't understand why we had laughed about it.

We hadn't seen a car outside, or heard one arrive, so we assumed that since they weren't on bicycles they must be on a walking holiday.

We were, therefore, astonished when they told us that they had started off from Glastonbury only that morning. They both then looked slightly puzzled when we congratulated them on their achievement. We told them that they must be very fit because they showed no signs of tiredness after their long journey.

'It was almost nothing,' said the man, with a shrug. 'We are a car very good German having. And I a skilful driver am.'

It turned out they had left their car in a farm gateway while they took a walk around the village; and that they had travelled no more than a quarter of mile on foot when they turned up at the Duck and Puddle.

We all felt very foolish and we were glad when they left. Frank, I remember, was particularly relieved to see the back of them.

'I felt nervous having them in the pub,' he whispered, checking to make sure that they'd really left the pub and were out of earshot.

We all looked at him, puzzled.

'Mind you,' he said, 'they were upfront about it. You've got to give them that.'

We were all still confused.

'They didn't look dangerous but I suppose you can never tell, can you? Some of these people get very good at hiding it.' He pulled an imaginary knife across his throat and shivered. 'And then all of sudden you find them slitting your throat for no reason at all. Just for them thinking you'd looked at them a bit funny.'

'Frank, how much have you had to drink?' asked Patchy.

'No more than the usual,' said Frank defiantly. This was back in the days when his 'usual' would have been enough to put most people into a coma.

'So, what the devil are you talking about?' Patchy asked.

'Them psychopaths,' said Frank. 'I'm talking about having that pair of psychopaths sitting in my pub.'

I remember, it took us nearly 20 minutes to explain to Frank that they weren't psychopaths or cyclists but psychics.'

'Oh, right,' said Frank, eventually. There was a long silence before the inevitable. 'So, what's a psychic do? Is there any future in it?'

But that was then and the two youths who were wearing khaki shorts had definitely arrived on bicycles. They each ordered a still lemonade and a ham sandwich. Frank tottered off to the Duck and Puddle kitchen to fulfil their order.

'It's quite a ride from Barnstaple,' said Thumper in a kindly tone. 'Where are you headed next?'

'We're going on to Lynmouth,' replied the tall cyclist. He managed to sound both defiant and defensive.

'That's some journey,' said Thumper. 'Are you staying there for the night?'

'No, no,' said the tall cyclist. 'We're going back to Barnstaple today.'

'Crumbs,' said Thumper. 'I'm very impressed.'

'Quite a round trip,' I said. I too was impressed. The distance between Barnstaple and Lynmouth might not be all that vast but the roads are not good and there are quite a number of hills to be climbed. I couldn't help wondering if the two youths knew what they were letting themselves in for. 'That road is very hilly,' I pointed out

'It won't be a problem for us,' said the tall cyclist, with a careless shrug. It seemed to me that he had all the false confidence of someone aged 13 or 14.

'If you are young and you believe in yourself you can do anything,' said the small youth with the scowl, now adding a sneer to the scowl. 'The trouble with older fogies like you lot is that you all think negatively.'

I thought this was a trifle unfair, ageist and inaccurate; and particularly inappropriate since my remarks had been well-intentioned.

Frank reappeared, carrying two large plates, upon each which lay a ham sandwich. 'Mustard?' he asked.

'No,' said the tall youth rudely. His smaller companion said nothing.

'You can do anything?' asked Patchy, putting the stress on the word anything.

'Of course!' replied the youth with all the confidence of a young man who has done very little and knows even less. 'Nothing is impossible if you simply have the will.'

'Really?'

'Of course!'

Frank returned with the two lemonades.

'Lift Frank up over your head while standing on one leg,' said Thumper.

'I beg your pardon?'

'You said you could do anything if you put your mind to it, so lift Frank over your head while standing on one leg.'

Frank looked rather alarmed at this but it was never going to happen. The youth with the scowl looked confused and then sniggered derisively.

'If that's too difficult then sing one of the arias from La bohème. Sing it in the original Italian, please.'

'Why?' demanded the youth.

'You said you could do anything,' Patchy pointed out quite accurately. He paused and held up two fingers. 'But you can't can you? So that's two things you can't do. We could go on all day thinking up things you can't do.'

I looked at Patchy. 'If La bohème has Italian lyrics, which I'm sure it has, why is the title of the opera in French?'

'Ah, that's a good question,' replied Patchy. 'The Italian libretto, which was written by two Italians, was sort of loosely based on a book called *Scenes de la vie de Boheme* which was written by a bloke called Henri Murger who was French.'

I was glad I asked.

The youth with the scowl was staring open mouthed at Patchy.

'The world premiere was held in Turin and conducted by a young fellow called Toscanini, of whom you may have heard,' said Patchy.

'So there was never much chance of the whole thing being written in another language, English say? Or Dutch?'

'Not really, no.'

'What's all that got to do with anything?' demanded the youth with the built in scowl. I got the feeling that he was aggrieved because he was now no longer the centre of attention.

'Absolutely nothing,' beamed Patchy.

The young cyclists turned their backs on us and concentrated on their sandwiches.

Half an hour later, having consumed their ham sandwiches (without mustard) and drunk their lemonade, the demon cyclists remounted their metallic steeds and set off to continue their journey to Lynmouth.

Sadly, it turned out that they had bitten off rather more than they could chew. Two days later, I heard that they had sought refuge at a bed and breakfast establishment in Parracombe and that on the following morning they had hitched a ride to Barnstaple on the back of a tractor drawn trailer. They and their bikes had been spotted by Thumper who said they looked like a very poor entry in the annual carnival at Withymoor.

'I used to ride a bicycle,' said Frank, when the pair had pedalled away.

We looked at him and stared in astonishment. I would, I think, have been less surprised if he'd told me that he'd seen a giraffe cycling around the Devon lanes.

'Get away with you!' said Thumper.

'No, I did,' insisted Frank. 'When I was a lad. It didn't have gears but it had a mudguard on the back and a little wire basket at the front. I used to deliver newspapers, groceries and pigeons.'

We stared at him, still struggling to come to terms with the idea of Frank riding a bicycle.

'I can understand the newspapers and the groceries,' said Patchy. 'But why pigeons?'

'A mate of my Dad's bred racing pigeons. I used to have to pedal out into the countryside and let the pigeons go at a particular time so that the bloke who owned them could see how long they took to get home. I was quite good on a bicycle,' continued Frank. 'I could ride for a little way without holding onto the handlebars.'

We were impressed.

'Not ridden one for years,' said Frank, thoughtfully. 'Not since the day I fell off. It's bloody painful when you fall off.'

'Did you hurt yourself?' asked Patchy.

'Landed on my head,' said Frank.

'Ah, that was probably the safest thing to do,' said Thumper, apparently solicitously.

Frank looked at him, slightly puzzled.

'Least likely to do any damage,' Thumper explained.

Frank frowned, thought for a moment and then threw his bar towel at Thumper's head.

Caleb's Ankle

Of course, not all visitors to the Duck and Puddle were as rude or as ungracious as the demon cyclists or the psychic Austrians.

The same day that the two demon cyclists called in on their way to Lynmouth, we had a visit from two of Frank's most long-standing customers: Bunty and Caleb Theodore.

Mr and Mrs Theodore were both in their late 80s and had been occasional regulars at the Duck and Puddle for donkey's years. They say they come for the sandwiches but I suspect they just enjoy our sparkling conversation and intelligent repartee.

(Frank defines an 'occasional regular' as someone who patronises the pub at intervals of more than a month between visits. Someone who visited the pub in 1957 and came back in 1972 would, in Frank's terms, be described as an 'occasional regular'. And so there are holidaymakers and tourists who visit Bilbury on an annual or biannual basis who can properly describe themselves as 'occasional regulars'.)

The Theodores live in West Bugford and to be honest they both looked their age when I first met them.

Caleb, who was reputedly once a Governor in one of Britain's few remaining colonies, had had two heart attacks and suffered a mild stroke which has left him with a hardly noticeable limp. He had recovered from cancer of the lung 20 years earlier and suffered from emphysema.

Over the years his wife, Bunty, had parted company with one breast, her uterus and both her ovaries. ('It's a damned effective way to lose weight,' she once said. On another occasion, she complained that there would soon be so much of her in the hospital incinerator that she would have to give that as her permanent address.) In her 20s, she developed diabetes and in her 70s she developed macular degeneration.

Caleb had a wobbly right leg and she had a dodgy left leg. They both used walking sticks, and for the past nine years had taken first prize in the three-legged race at the village sports day.

But they didn't think or behave like people who were within hailing distance of their century and they certainly didn't think or behave like people who were inclined to be aware of their mortality.

They were as full of life as anyone half a century younger.

Their attitude seemed to be: 'Come here, Life! You've given me as good as you can. Now, it's your turn. Take this, that and this.'

The lives of too many of the older folk I have met have been dominated by their things they meant to do, wanted to do, never got round to doing or did and now regret.

Caleb and Bunty, on the other hand, had filled their lives with so many ideas, plans, hopes and ambitions that any failings and fears which might have defined their lives were effectively smothered and unable to take a hold on their memories.

For most of us, it is our fears and regrets which define the people we become; it is our fears which come back in the night, like ghosts, and which terrorise our lives. It is our regrets which interfere with our ambitions so that instead of looking forward we are forever peering over our shoulders at the past. Caleb and Bunty were so occupied with tomorrow that they never had time for yesterday.

They had interests and enthusiasms galore.

For example, they were both keen gardeners and on one occasion when I visited them, they showed me around their amazing garden. To my astonishment, they pointed out a number of plants which were named after parts of the human body. I remember they showed me lady's-tresses (a type of orchid) liverwort and navelwort. (At the end of this book, there is an appendix in which I have, with Caleb's help, listed some of the many plants which are named after bits and pieces of the human body.)

Despite their advanced years and their fraility, Caleb and Bunty were always full of ideas and energy and over the months, they used to come to the Duck and Puddle to sit in the Snug and discuss their latest plans. Retirement is, of course, an entirely artificial concept and it was not an idea which Caleb and Bunty had given any consideration; they were serial entrepreneurs and risk was in their blood.

Some of their plans were quite fantastic and wildly unworkable. But several of them were definitely practical.

I learnt a great deal from them – not least the best way to deal with administrators and bureaucrats.

It was Caleb who taught me that it was possible to cause great chaos in government departments, utility companies and large multinational organisations by carefully preparing your correspondence.

So, for example, you could say (see page 2) at the bottom of page 1 but then just put page1 into the envelope all alone. The recipient would think they had lost page 2 and would eventually write back asking for the missing information. Or you could put in a reference to a Mr Harrison who 'in his letter referring to his matter pointed out that…'. There would, of course, be no Mr Harrison.

These small tricks added a frisson of entertainment to tedious correspondence and, Caleb pointed out, often helped to derail a bureaucratic investigation.

Sadly, these tricks don't work these days. No one working for a government department, utility company or large multinational organisation ever reads any mail – let alone bothers to reply to it.

Still, they were fun while they lasted.

I've forgotten the details of many of the business proposals put forward by the Theodores, but I do remember that we all got terribly excited when they talked to us about setting up a gambling ship in the Bristol Channel. They believed, quite wrongly as it turned out, that if they anchored a ship in the middle of the Channel they would be far enough outside territorial waters to be able to avoid all the relevant legislation. They had seen a movie in which American gangsters had organised a similar scheme with great success and they'd rather hoped to try the idea in the waters off Ilfracombe. Sadly, this was an idea which was not of its time.

And then there was the theme park they wanted to set up to celebrate Sherlock Holmes and his loyal companion Dr Watson. Their plan was to purchase and renovate a tumble down manor house on Dartmoor. They hoped to build a museum and a library and to hire actors to play Sherlock Holmes, Dr John Watson, Professor Moriaty, Mycroft Holmes, Inspector Lestrade, Mrs Hudson and Irene Adler. And they also intended to hold 'mystery' weekends where visitors could join Sherlock Holmes and Dr Watson as they attempted to solve 'a case'. They planned to dress up a Great Dane to play the part of the Baskerville's notorious hound.

That project got quite close to realisation but fell quite late on when planning officials refused to countenance necessary changes to the old manor house they were hoping to restore. In the end, no one could think of anything else to do with it and so the old manor house had to be demolished so I suppose we can chalk that one up as another 'victory' for planning nonsenses. I never got round to visiting the Manor House but I saw photographs and it was a marvellously scary looking place.

Caleb once told me that most people assume that the folk in authority know what they are doing. This, he said, is wrong. 'The people in authority may know what you are doing and they almost certainly know what I am doing but they don't have the faintest idea what they themselves are doing.'

On another occasion, the Theodores got quite close to opening a nightclub in Ilfracombe. Their plan was to create a club which looked like a pirates' hideout, complete with seating designed to look like fake treasure chests and a bar selling many different varieties of rum. The nightclub failed at a late-stage hurdle when the Theodores were gazumped and the empty building they were hoping to purchase was bought by a hungry supermarket chain looking for a site where they could sell tins of baked beans and boxes of washing powder.

At one time, the couple wanted to open a pub in South Molton.

Their marketing ploy was to give the pub a name that would give businessmen and businesswomen a chance to go and have a drink without their colleagues knowing what they were getting up to. And so they planned to call their pub something like 'The Gym' or 'My Accountant's Office', thus enabling customers to say, with perfect honesty, 'I'm just off to the gym' or 'I must pop along to my accountant's office'.

Bunty planned to dress the barmaids in low cut blouses and high cut skirts (designed to be just low enough and high enough to delight the male customers without upsetting the female ones) and to dress a couple of barmen in sailor outfits, even equipping them with little sailor hats. Her plan was that these would prove an attraction for female customers though, as Thumper pointed out, there was an excellent chance that the sailor boys might turn out to attract a certain sort of male customer rather than to prove a magnet for heterosexual women.

None of this mattered, however, for this brilliant plan failed at the last minute not because of the sailor hats but because a brewery chain opened a new pub next door to the site where the Theodores had intended to open their public house. The brewery called their pub 'The Smuggler's Rest', (a name which should have won them some sort of prize for unoriginality) and equipped it with half an acre of red plastic and two dozen old hunting prints. 'The Smuggler's Rest' was a success only because the brewery sold its own beer at half price in order to undercut, and destroy, the competition.

Not all of Caleb and Bunty's proposed business schemes ended in failure.

On the contrary, a number of their projects managed to get all the way to fruition and were astonishing successes.

So, for example, they opened a novelty miniature golf course in Westward Ho! This turned out to be enormously popular with holidaymakers and was for many years something of a money spinner for them, helping to pay for them to pursue some of their other dreams.

And they opened the first new cinema to be built in North Devon for as long as anyone could remember. They converted a warehouse which had stood empty for years and had it fitted out with second-hand seats and an old screen which they had brought down from somewhere in Scotland. Their 'unique selling point' was that the cinema would show old classic movies; mostly shot in black and white. That too proved to be very popular with holidaymakers, particularly on rainy days.

I remember Bunty, Caleb, Thumper, Patchy, Gilly, Frank, Patsy and I all spending a Sunday afternoon discussing names for the new cinema.

Caleb had a wonderful old dictionary which enabled him to tell us that the word Odeon was originally devised to describe a theatre for musical contests in ancient Greece and Rome, that the word Hippodrome was originally used to denote an open air course for horse and chariot racing and that the word Alhambra described a palace built for the Moorish kings in Granada and Spain.

We took a vote on what the cinema should be named and agreed on The Alhambra. We all thought the name had the gravitas required to give status to a crumbling warehouse.

Six months later, the cinema was up and running and showing the marvellous *Thin Man* films, starring William Powell and Myrna Loy. The Theodores followed this with a season of Bogart movies.

Sadly, the cinema eventually had to close.

I never knew why but Thumper always reckoned it was because someone on the local council found out that locals and visitors had been spotted enjoying themselves. I suspect there may have been some truth in this. I doubt if Caleb and Bunty made any money out of the cinema but they certainly had a lot of fun with it.

'So, what's new?' asked Thumper, when the Theodores walked in.

(I suppose, if I am honest which I always am, I have to admit that to say that they 'walked in' is rather misleading in that it implies a sense of certainty, determination and speed and none of these could be used to describe the Theodore's progress. There was a certain amount of hobbling and limping involved whenever the Theodores (particularly Caleb) chose to move from A to B, and progress was always on the stationary side of slow.)

As usual, despite their years, neither of them was wearing anything beige or made with useful Velcro attachments or elasticated sides.

Bunty was wearing a flowered print skirt in yellow and green, a beautiful yellow blouse and green shoes. She had her hair cut in what is, I think, called a pageboy bob. It was dyed blonde and had a purple streak on one side which gave her a gaily piratical air.

Caleb was wearing bottle green cavalry twill trousers and a stylish jacket in red corduroy. He wore a multi-coloured shirt and a Marylebone Cricket Club tie which clashed with the shirt and everything else he was wearing, though, of course, it is an acknowledged fact of sartorial life that a bacon and egg coloured MCC tie clashes with most colour schemes. The tie was perfectly tied in a Windsor knot, with the two ends nicely aligned. Whenever I try to tie a Windsor knot, I end up with one end of the tie three or four inches longer than the other. This never seemed to happen to Caleb.

'We came to pick your brains,' said Bunty.

They didn't bother to order drinks because Frank new exactly what they wanted: a small cherry brandy for her and half a pint of Guinness for him. In addition, she would have two packets of salted peanuts and he would have a packet of pork scratchings. Then, half an hour later, they would each have a couple of Frank's enormous sandwiches.

'In that case, are you sure you came to the right place?' asked Frank, over his shoulder.

Bunty ignored him. 'Caleb is having trouble with his foot,' she said. 'His own GP has made an appointment for him to go back to the Prosthetics Clinic but there's a nine week waiting list.'

'We wondered if you fellows had any bright ideas,' said Caleb.

Frank brought their drinks, together with the peanuts and the pork scratchings.

I think I forget to mention earlier that during the Second World War, Caleb lost his right leg below the knee. Ever since then he's used a rather old-fashioned and very heavy prosthesis; partly made of metal and partly made of wood. The experts had on many occasions tried to persuade him to upgrade to a more modern, lighter prosthesis but Caleb was attached to his old, faithful foot and calf. He said he'd got used to it and, at his time of life, didn't want to spend time breaking in a new prosthesis. He certainly got around moderately well with it.

At his suggestion, I took a look at the faulty leg.

'One of the bolts holding my foot onto my shin has sheared,' said Caleb. 'The result is that the whole foot wobbles about a bit.' He waggled his foot and for a moment I thought it was going to fall off. He had effected a very temporary repair with a piece of metal which looked as though it had been taken from a broken door bolt.

'I got the temporary piece of metal from a broken door bolt,' said Caleb, when he saw me examining the repair.

'We've got a wedding next Saturday,' said Bunty. 'Our granddaughter is getting married. Caleb's terribly worried that his foot will fall off at an inopportune moment.'

It occurred to me that I couldn't think of an opportune moment for a foot to fall off. But I didn't say anything. 'This should be in a museum,' I told him, poking at the faulty prosthesis. It really was very old. There were signs of rust on the metal parts and what looked like woodworm holes in the wooden part.

'That's where it's going when I've finished with it,' said Caleb rather proudly. 'When I snuff it, the hospital people are going to put the whole caboodle into their collection of ancient prostheses.'

'Meanwhile,' I said, 'it seems absurd that you should have to wait more than two months to have your dodgy joint mended.'

'Reggie,' said Thumper suddenly.

We all looked at him.

'Reggie Westbury,' explained Thumper. 'At Tolstoys.'

Tolstoys is, for reasons far too complicated to explain, the name of our local garage.

'A garage?' I said. 'How can the garage help?'

'Reggie makes a lot of car parts,' explained Thumper. 'I bet he could easily make a bolt for Caleb's ankle joint.'

Five of us went round to Tolstoy's garage together. Thumper, Patchy and I led the way in the Rolls and Caleb and Bunty followed in their Morris Minor. Frank had to stay in the Duck and Puddle in case any other customers turned up.

It took Reginald less than 30 minutes to make a new bolt for Caleb's ankle joint.

I've rarely seen anyone quite as delighted. It is no exaggeration to say that Caleb was tickled pink, over the moon and as pleased as Punch. 'That's marvellous!' he said. 'I'll ring the doctor tomorrow and tell him to cancel the appointment at the clinic. How much do I owe you?'

'Five shillings will cover it,' said Reginald, who had not at that time adapted to Britain's decimal currency. Five shillings was 25 pence.

'Cheap at twice the price,' said Caleb, taking out his wallet.

'Ok, ten shillings then,' said Reginald.

Caleb, clearly surprised, looked at him.

'Don't be daft,' said Reginald. 'Five bob is fine.'

Caleb then insisted on taking us back to the Duck and Puddle to celebrate.

He didn't mind a bit that the celebrations cost him rather more than the repair.

The Bathroom Cabinet

I looked at the pieces of chipboard laid out on the drawing room floor and scratched my head. There were, and I had counted them, 18 pieces of artificial wood, 28 funny little bits of metal of a size and variety I had never seen before, and a large, mixed plastic bag full of screws and catches. There was an exploded diagram which looked as if it were a map of the Tokyo transport system after a successful air raid attack. And there was a small tube of glue which had printed on the side a warning not to get any of the stuff on your skin. 'In event on skin contacting telephone doctor straightway.' This rather alarmed me since 'in event on skin contacting' I would be consulting myself and I didn't have the foggiest idea what I should tell myself. There was no information on the tube about the nature of the contents.

Oh, and there was an instruction booklet too.

Not that the instruction booklet was much good. It had either been written in a foreign language and then translated into English by a first year language student or else it had been written by a half-witted sadist with an unusual sense of humour.

I looked again at the paragraph I had been attempting to understand.

'Place the rocheted console bracket under PIECE AA and connect PIECE G to PIECE HH with the aid of one of the small congealant screws and wash with connection adjustable type OO using the tool provided and then while holding PIECE AA and PIECE EE with PIECE M put bracket lock against console base and use fixator clip to console PIECE F on side of left side of cabinet with fixator screwings against wall connection bracketing to adjust the PIECE MO towards back of side of cabinet against fixed lock with securing tool with fixator clip and adjust screwings against door at point JJ on plan with screwing tool before adjusting to match width of PIECE R.'

I read the paragraph silently, I read it aloud and then I held it on its side and tried to read it with one eye closed. I then read it to Ben, the dog, who listened attentively but who didn't seem to understand it any better than I had. I then wandered around the house until I found Patsy and I read it to her. She laughed and thought I'd made it up but then I showed her the booklet and she knew I hadn't made it up and she got quite cross and said how very silly it was that anyone should print such rubbish.

The bits and pieces laid out on the drawing room floor were supposed to be a bathroom cupboard but I didn't see how they could ever become a bathroom cabinet or, indeed, anything more sophisticated than a basket of kindling.

I went back downstairs, found the advertisement which contained the telephone number of the company from which I had purchased the cupboard, and rang them up.

'In the advertisement which I saw, and to which I responded, the cupboard looks like a cupboard,' I said when someone finally answered the telephone. 'But you've sent me a construction set. Is my cupboard supposed to be all in bits or did it fall apart in the mail?'

'We send out all our furniture in a consumer friendly deconstructed format. This enables us to maximise product functionability and to minimise cost.'

'I wish you'd told me that I was going to have to make the thing myself.'

'If you look carefully at our advertisement you will see that we state in the small print that we believe in package minimalisation and so, as a result, we offer all our furniture in a user friendly deconstructed format.'

I looked at the advertisement and there it was, in the small print at the bottom of the page. 'We believe in package minimalisation. For the convenience of our customers, all our furniture is supplied in a user friendly deconstructed format.'

'How is it more convenient for me to have to build it myself?' I demanded.

'If it arrived ready-made it would be a very large and cumbersome package and because of the weight you might have difficulty lifting it.'

'It would weigh exactly the same!'

'Yes, but it would be larger and more cumbersome.'

'If I'd known I was going to have to build it myself I wouldn't have bought it!' I said rather crossly.

'Do you have a reference number for the item in question?' asked the woman with a weary sounding sigh.

I looked at the box and found the reference number, which was stamped on the outside of the package. 'The reference number appears to be DEGM483736.'

'Was that BCEN483736?'

'No, no. It's DEGM483736.'

'B for Bravo?'

'No! D for Diarrhoea.'

'Oh, you mean D for Delta?'

'D for Diarrhoea will do.'

'Oh no! It should be D for Delta. And then it was C for Charlie?'

'No, it's E for Earache.'

'You mean E for Echo?'

I was getting fed up with this. 'Why can't it be E for Earache?'

'It has to be E for Echo.'

'But Earache also begins with an E. And Earache is just as good a word as Echo. In fact I don't mind betting that people use the word Earache more than they use the word Echo."

'It has to be E for Echo. It cannot be E for Earache. I have Echo written down on a special list. Everyone has to use the special list.'

I wrote down E for Earache on the back of the leaflet that had come with the bathroom cupboard.

'Well, I've got E for Earache written down here,' I said.

'No, you have to use the same list as I use,' she said sniffily. 'And the third letter of your reference number is E for Echo?'

'No, the third letter of my reference number is G for Gastritis. Or, if you prefer, it could be G for Gallstones.'

'G for Golf,' said the woman.

We argued about this for a while.

'And the fourth letter,' said the woman, who was beginning to sound slightly hysterical. 'Would that be N for November?'

'No. It would be M for Metatarsophalangeal.'

'I beg your pardon?'

'M for Metatarsophalangeal.'

'Is that rude? It sounds rude.' She was clearly preparing herself to be offended. Some people like to be offended so that they can take offence.

'No, it's certainly not rude. It refers to the joints between the metatarsal bones of the foot.'

'Well, it should be M for Mike.'

'Who is Mike?'

'I don't know who Mike is. But it should be M for Mike.'

'Why not M for Michelle? Or M for Miranda? Or M for Maurice?'

'I don't know. But it's M for Mike.'

'It could just as well be M for Muscles. Yes, definitely. It is M for Muscles.'

Eventually, we agreed on the reference number although not on what the letters stood for. The numbers were easy.

'Is the product you purchased the two-seater, foam cushioned garden swing seat with adjustable springs?' she asked, presumably having compared the reference number on which we had agreed with her product list.

'No. It's a bathroom cabinet.'

'Are you absolutely certain it isn't a garden swing seat?'

'Pretty sure. It doesn't look much like a bathroom cabinet but I'm pretty confident you could never make a garden swing seat out of these bits and pieces.'

'Well, according to our records your product is a garden swing seat. You must be mistaken. Never mind, it doesn't matter. All our products have the same five year guarantee and customer friendly policy regarding returns. You can take advantage of our returns policy for this product by following the instructions on the back page of the construction leaflet accompanying your item.'

I looked at the back page of the leaflet.

'It says that I can return the item as long as the packaging is complete and unopened.'

'That's correct.'

'But if I hadn't opened the package I wouldn't have been able to get hold of the leaflet telling me your returns policy.'

'If you have opened the package in which your garden swing seat came, then I'm afraid you will have damaged the packaging and so you can no longer return it for a refund.'

'Even though I had to open the package to discover your returns policy? That's utter madness! And it's a bathroom cabinet not a garden swing seat.'

'It is our policy, to protect customers in this way.'

'How does this protect customers?'

'If we allowed people to return damaged goods our prices would have to rise and customers would suffer.'

'And it's not even painted!' I protested. 'In the photograph on your advertisement the cupboard is clearly painted white.'

'We like to give our customers the freedom to paint their cupboard in a colour of their choice.'

'Is it safe to burn it?' I asked.

'I beg your pardon?'

'If I burn the bits and pieces will they produce toxic fumes?'

'Are you intending to burn your garden seat?'

'Yes, I think I am.'

'Your warranty will not be valid if you have damaged it in any way. Burning it would definitely invalidate the warranty.'

'But the warranty is invalidated because I opened the packaging.'

'Yes. That is to protect our customers.'

I put down the telephone receiver and then I counted to ten. When I had counted to ten I screamed, stamped on the disconnected bathroom cabinet and ripped the instruction leaflet into shreds.'

'What's up?' asked Patsy, suddenly appearing, attracted by the noise I was making. 'Are you all right?'

'This is our new bathroom cabinet,' I explained, pointing to the bits and pieces which were now scattered across the drawing room floor. 'I'm going to burn it.'

'Oh,' said Patsy. 'That's nice.'

She looked at the scattered bits of artificial wood and the strange pieces of metal. 'My cousin used to have one of those building sets when he was little. He once made a small windmill with little vanes that went round if you gave them a push.'

'This is all going on the bonfire,' I told her. 'Heaven knows what chemicals this stuff contains. I'll set fire to it and then run for safety.'

'I don't know why you didn't just ask Patchy,' said Patsy, with great common sense. 'He could probably find us a very nice bathroom cabinet for half the price and none of the effort.'

As usual, she was right, of course.

After I'd thrown the bits and pieces onto my bonfire site, I went round to see Patchy. The assorted screws and bits of metal I threw into the dustbin.

I found my friend and brother-in-law in his workshop at the back of the garage he uses as a gallery. He was busy bending over a large painting of a woman on a chair. He had a paintbrush in his hand.

'I'm just putting the wedding ring back,' he said, stepping back and examining the painting from further away. 'What do you think?'

'It's not a terribly good painting, is it?'

'No, but what do you think of the wedding ring? Convincing?'

'Very,' I agreed. 'She definitely looked married.'

'Good.'

'May I ask why you are painting on a wedding ring and turning a maiden lady into a married woman?'

'She originally had a wedding ring on but I painted over it.'

'Why on earth did you do that?' I asked. 'Is that usual? Would you paint a wedding ring on the Mona Lisa?'

'Probably not,' said Patchy. 'But this isn't exactly the Mona Lisa.'

'No, I suppose not.'

'I bought it cheap at an auction in Taunton and I had a couple of possible buyers but they didn't like the wedding ring. A lot of people who buy paintings of women prefer to think of the woman in the picture as being a young girl, a spinster. Men want to fall in love with her and women want to treat her as a daughter.'

'So you painted out the wedding ring?'

'Yes. But they still didn't buy it. One said he'd never be able to forget that she was really married and the other decided he didn't like the look of her after all.'

'So, why are you putting the ring back in?'

'Because I've got a buyer who collects paintings of famous women and I'm going to tell him that this is Mrs Pankhurst. So she obviously needs a wedding ring.'

'Is it Mrs Pankhurst? It doesn't look a lot like her.'

'It doesn't look anything like her,' admitted Patchy. 'But a lot of Victorian portraits don't much look like the people they are supposed to represent. I'll explain that she was having a bad day. Or that the artist was having a bad day.' He picked up a small, brass coloured plaque engraved with the words 'Mrs Emily Pankhurst' and began to screw it to the bottom of the gold frame.

'Where on earth did you get that?'

'Thumper had it made for me. He's got a pal who does engraving.'

Patchy put the second screw in and stood back. The picture now did look convincing, and with the nameplate in place, I would have believed that it was a portrait of Mrs Pankhurst.

'Have you got any bathroom cabinets for sale?' I asked.

'What's that got to do with Victorian portrait paintings and Mrs Pankhurst?'

'Nothing whatsoever. But I want to buy a bathroom cabinet. Somewhere to put toothbrushes and soap and stuff like that. I bought one of those modern things they advertise in the newspapers. But now that it's arrived I've got to build it.'

Patchy looked at me and shuddered. 'I wish you wouldn't tell me things like that,' he said. He thought for a moment, mentally going through his stock I suppose, and then shook his head. 'I haven't got anything that would serve as a bathroom cabinet. But there's an auction in Lynton starting in about 40 minutes. There's a lot of Victorian and Edwardian brown furniture in the sale. They're bound to have a bathroom cabinet or something that will serve as a bathroom cabinet.'

'Did the Victorians have bathroom cabinets?'

'Of course they did. Old bathroom furniture tends to go quite cheaply. You can probably get one for a fiver.'

I rang Patsy to tell her where I could be found, and off we went to Lynton.

On the way, Patchy told me about an auction he had been to in Exeter.

It had been what is known as a 'time auction', in which the auctioneer allows a specific amount of time for the sale of each lot. Patchy told me that auctioneers sometimes do this simply to add excitement to a sale. So, for example, the time limit might be three minutes. At the end of the three minutes, the item being sold is marked down to the person who is the highest bidder at that moment. The 'time auction' can apparently produce some very hectic bidding as the time runs out. Patchy said that auctioneers in France have a variation on this type of auction. They light a candle at the start of the auction and the proceedings end when the candle goes out.

The prize lot in this particular 'time auction' was a rusty, old car; an ancient vehicle which had been found in the barn of a house on the Devon-Cornwall border. The owner of the car had become a recluse and hadn't left his home for nearly 40 years. His abandoned motor vehicle, which was spattered with bird guano, was a Bugatti Type 37and Patchy had, of course, dreamt of buying it for a song. Rare cars found in barns seem to come up at auction with monotonous regularity.

Sadly, Patchy's hopes were dashed by the fact that the auctioneer had done his job properly and had promoted the car to the motor trade. As a result, there were two specialist car dealers at the auction. Patchy's top bid had been passed without the two dealers getting out of first gear and the final selling price had been five times Patchy's potential top price and three times the estimate listed in the catalogue.

'Still,' said Patchy, with a smile, 'at least I can say that I got to bid on a barn find Bugatti. And I was the second under-bidder too.'

The auction in Lynton was held in what looked like, and probably once was, a shed. It had corrugated iron walls and a corrugated iron roof which appeared to be held in place by hope and bits of baler twine. The place was packed to where the rafters would have been if there had been any. There were wardrobes, tables, chairs, sideboards and bookcases galore.

'Where does all this stuff come from?' I asked Patchy, surprised, as always, at the amount of stuff that was on sale.

He shrugged. 'Most of it just goes round and round,' he admitted. 'One dealer will buy a job lot of stuff and then sell it to another at a second auction, hoping to make a few quid. Or hoping that an American buyer will take the lot and send it over to the States. An awful lot of the stuff that appears in auction rooms is never bought by a house owner and probably never used. But it's all good, solid furniture and, sadly for us, the Americans seem to appreciate our heritage more than we do.' He pointed to a dark oak cabinet, about four feet high and the same in width. 'There you are,' he said, 'one bathroom cabinet in good condition.'

We checked out the cabinet and I had to agree that it was perfect for our purposes. Patchy wrote down the lot number on his catalogue and then examined what looked to me to be a rather ropey old long case clock – the sort I usually think of as a grandfather clock.

'It doesn't seem to be working,' I pointed out. 'And there's a hand missing!'

'I know a man who can probably get it working,' whispered Patchy. 'And it only ever had one hand. Early clocks only had one hand. It was common as late as the 17th century and the early 18th century for clockmakers to produce clocks with just one hand. People who lived in country areas didn't really need a minute hand. A single hour hand was perfectly satisfactory. This clock has a brass dial which means it was probably made between 1680 and 1770 and from the spandrels on the dial I can tell it was made outside London, probably at the end of the 17th century or the very beginning of the 18th century.'

'What's a spandrel?'

'The fancy markings at the four corners of the clock face,' said Patchy, peering at the dial which was black with dirt. 'There you are,' he said pointing to a word on the dial, 'it was made in Newport.'

'Is it valuable?'

'It's probably worth more than I'll have to pay for it,' said Patchy, looking around the auction room. 'I can't see anyone here who deals in clocks. Most of the people here will be looking to fill their vans with a consignment of brown furniture. Some of it will end up in a dealer's shop in London, some of it will end up in an auction house in New York and some of it will end up at another auction here in the West Country.'

Patchy also found a box containing a collection of old books and he became surprisingly excited by one of the oldest books, a particularly scruffy item, which had a metal ring fitted to one corner.

'That's not what I think it is, is it?' I said.

As a bibliophile I knew a little about the history of books. I had seen chained books in the library at Hereford Cathedral but I hadn't ever picked one up before.

'It certainly is,' murmured Patchy, picking out the book and carefully opening it. 'It's a book which used to be on the shelf in a chained library.'

Up until the end of the 17th century, it was rare to find a printed book in an English household. William Caxton, who ran the Caxton Press in Westminster is famous for having been the first ever printer in England but he only produced just over 100 books during 15 years of work between 1477 and 1491. You'd have thought a busy monk could have written out that many by hand. The inevitable result was that books were scarce and even second-hand ones were extremely valuable. Only the biggest churches, universities and wealthy gentlemen could afford libraries and it was, therefore, the usual practice to keep books chained up. This allowed readers to consult the books in a library but it made it difficult for anyone to steal them. The books were stored with their spines at the back of the shelf, so that they could be taken out and read without the chain getting into a tangle.

'So how old is that one?' I asked.

'It's not that old,' said Patchy, rather disappointed. 'It's a dictionary and according to the copyright line inside, it was printed in 1871. Chained libraries were dying out by then.'

'Valuable?'

'Not as valuable as if it had been printed in the Middle Ages!' laughed Patchy. He put the book back into the box from which he had taken it and then covered it with some other old books – most of them reprints of 19th century novels and cookery books. 'We'll bid on the boxful,' he said. 'Probably get the whole lot for a quid.'

Thanks to Patchy we both had a good day.

Patchy got the clock for £55, I got the sturdy bathroom cabinet for £4.50 (less than the do-it-yourself cupboard I had abandoned) and Patchy bought the box of books for 50 pence. When we got back outside the auction room, he presented me with the chained book as a present.

And when we got back to Bilbury, he helped me carry the bathroom cabinet up into the bathroom. It looked far better, and far more in keeping with the house, than the wretched piece of flimsy make-it-yourself nonsense which I had failed to build.

Returning the compliment, I then went back to his gallery cum showroom cum garage to help him unload the grandfather clock from his truck.

We had just successfully moved the clock into the workshop at the back of the gallery when the buyer who had expressed an interest in the painting of Mrs Pankhurst arrived to take a look at it.

'That's not her!' said the woman instantly.

'No?' said Patchy. 'How can you be so sure?'

'That woman is wearing a wedding ring,' said the woman sternly. 'Emily Pankhurst did not wear a wedding ring. I've seen many photographs of her.'

'Maybe the artist made a mistake,' said Patchy.

'That picture is a fake!' said the woman. And with that she stormed out.

'Bugger,' sighed Patchy, when she'd gone. 'If I hadn't painted the wedding ring on her finger I'd have sold the damned thing.'

'Never mind,' I said. 'You'll think of someone else she could be.'

Patchy brightened up. 'Of course I will! Do you think the woman in the picture looks anything like Florence Nightingale?'

'But you'll have to paint out that wedding ring.'

'Easily done,' said Patchy, reaching for his paints and his brush.

The woman in the picture would soon become a maiden lady again.

Caught in the Rocks

It was a good afternoon for staying indoors, lighting a log fire, toasting some muffins and settling down with a good book.

The day had started with promise. The sun had been out, the sky had been blue, decorated with just a few fluffy, white clouds, and a gentle breeze, a veritable zephyr in poetic terms, had promised to keep the day a pleasant temperature.

I'd finished the surgery earlier than usual and done the day's home visits by lunchtime. Patsy and I had eaten in the garden, where we have a huge, solid oak table and half a dozen matching chairs. The table and the chairs came from an auction and Patchy reckons they are at least 75-years-old. Occasionally, when I look at them, I find myself wondering how much modern garden furniture will still be functioning and looking good in three quarters of a century time.

But shortly after lunch the weather had changed, and it had changed rapidly.

The first sign of the impending change had come when our pet sheep had suddenly started to run for the barn, where they are accustomed to shelter from hot sun, rain, wind, snow and any other weather they don't like.

A good many animals, both small and large, can predict the weather.

The common or garden woodlouse may be small but he is remarkably prescient. He knows it is going to rain 24 hours before the first spots of rain start to fall, and he will respond by coming indoors to shelter. I don't believe that sheep know what the weather is going to do that far in advance but they certainly know a good 20 to 30 minutes before humans do.

'We'd better move everything indoors,' said Patsy.

I looked up from the magazine I was reading.

'It's going to rain.'

And then I too saw the sheep running for the barn.

We moved everything into the kitchen and Patsy put the coffee percolator onto the stove. When we'd done this I looked outside. The sun was still shining but there were now a few more clouds in the sky and it was clear that they were moving with a little more enthusiasm than had previously been the case. When I looked to the west, I could see a couple of large, nasty looking grey clouds on the horizon. The sheep had, as usual, been accurate. I settled down in the drawing room with my magazine, though I was close to nodding off.

I'd had a long, hard night and hadn't slept at all.

One of my patients, Mrs Daisy Marsh had an asthma attack and I stayed with her for an hour and a half while she gradually recovered.

When I go out on calls at night, I always leave the address and phone number of where I'll be on a pad by the telephone. This means that if another emergency call comes in, Patsy can telephone and pass on the message.

Just as I finished dealing with Mrs Marsh, Patsy phoned and told me I was needed at a cottage on the other side of the village. Mr Arthur Moe had woken up with muscular spasms in his back.

I managed to sort out Mr Moe's problem but ten minutes after I got back to Bilbury Grange there was a request to visit Fanny Murray, a small child who had woken up with earache. It took me no more than a minute to make the diagnosis, and less than five minutes to hand out the necessary medicines and reassure the parents. But by the time I got back home it really wasn't worth going to bed. I had breakfast, sorted through some correspondence and then did the morning surgery and visits.

Thankfully, I don't often have so many calls in one night.

And so, as a result of a night without sleep, I was now having difficulty in keeping my eyes open. The smell of the coffee Patsy was preparing was the only thing keeping me awake. Outside I could hear the first sounds of rain hammering on the windows. This was clearly going to be quite a storm. I was relieved to be tucked safely and cosily indoors. And I had two wonderful, free hours before the evening surgery was due to start; plenty of time for a leisurely coffee, a look at the book I was reading and maybe even a little proof reading of the book I had just finished writing. The two hours stretched out ahead of me welcomingly.

And then the telephone rang.

Oh, how I sometimes loathed that damned machine and how I cursed Alexander Graham Bell. Why couldn't he have invented something that didn't interrupt my life with such a savage and imperious urgency? There are lots of other things he could have invented instead: a machine for picking apples without bruising them; a motor car tyre that never punctures; a pen that never runs out of ink.

Most people can, of course, switch on their telephone answering machine if they wish to escape from the demands of their telephone. But the country GP has no access to such a simple luxury. He might as well be tied to the telephone by an umbilical cord. Whenever I go anywhere, I have to tell Patsy or Miss Johnson where I am going to be.

I have never for an instant wished for another life.

I am forever conscious of the joy of living and working in Bilbury. I regard myself as being the luckiest man alive, and having the very best job in the world.

But occasionally, just occasionally, I did find myself wishing that Mr Bell had invented something other than the telephone. It had already been one of those days which are several sizes too small.

I picked up the telephone receiver and answered with the number.

'Thank heavens you're there, doctor,' said a breathless voice which I immediately recognised.

The voice belonged to Bertram Brimstone who, in the summer months, when there are plenty of walkers, hikers and tourists about, runs an ice cream van in a car park near to Heddon's Mouth. In the winter he helps make and find the stock which his wife, Bertha, sells on the market stall she has in Barnstaple's famous Pannier Market. She sells home-made greeting cards, old postcards, second-hand books (mostly cheap paperbacks), old vinyl records and just about anything else which isn't too heavy. Everything they have on their stall has to be carried there from the back of the ice cream van which they use as a transport vehicle.

Surprisingly, Bertram (never Bertie) makes the home-made greeting cards himself. He buys old birthday and Christmas cards from nursing homes, hospitals and other similar institutions (paying just pennies per dozen) and then cuts up the cards so that he can use the pictures to create new cards. He sticks the pictures he has cut out onto pieces of thick paper. I don't honestly see how this time consuming activity can possibly be profitable but they've both been doing it for years so I suppose they must be able to make it worthwhile. Indeed, this bizarre form of recycling seems to be a small cottage industry in North Devon.

Bertram used to have a small boat which he kept at Combe Martin. In the summer, he would take visitors for a short, 30 minute trip along the coast. But, sadly, it wasn't very profitable. Bertram is living proof of the adage that for boat owners, the second happiest day of their life is the day when they bought their boat and the happiest is the day when they've finally managed to sell it and begin the long, slow journey back towards becoming a landlubber again.

Patsy and I have often thought of buying a small boat but the madness has fortunately always left us before it could turn into reality. Boats look good and seem fun until you have to wash them, ream the gribble worms out of the keel, caulk the windlass, splice the spinnaker, keelhaul the main brace, varnish the bulwarks, clean out the bilges, grease the propeller shaft, polish the brass and clear away the barnacles.

A friend of ours who had a boat for five years, reckons he spent 20 hours scrubbing and polishing and scraping, and five hours trying to remove grease from his hands, for every hour he spent at sea.

Bertram, who is usually a calm and laid back sort of fellow, sounded to be in a panic. He was certainly out of breath.

'Can you come quickly, doctor.'

'What's up, Bertram?' I asked. I had never before heard him so distressed.

'There's a man stuck in the rocks,' he said. He sounded breathless. 'And the tide is coming in.'

'Whereabouts?' I asked. The North Devon coast extends for some miles.

'Heddon's Mouth.'

'Oh,' I said.

This was bad news. Heddon's Mouth is a small, attractive cove which can only be reached by a meandering footpath which runs alongside the River Heddon through the Heddon Valley. The river ends at a small rock strewn beach, where the river flows into the sea. The route to the beach is a couple of miles long and usually takes walkers an hour or so. Even if you hurried, it would take a good half an hour. There is no road access at all and it is probably the worst place on the coast to be stuck in rocks. 'Have you called the fire brigade?'

'They say they can't get here for an hour,' said Bertram. 'All their engines are at a fire in Torrington. A pub is ablaze and they've still got people trapped. But they'll send someone as soon as they can.'

'The ambulance service?'

'They said they'll be three quarters of an hour at best,' said Bertram. 'And even if they get here, they can't get down to the cove in one of their ambulances. The poor devil is going to drown. You can hear his screams half a mile away. He's just screaming and sobbing. His wife and kids are all down there too. They're screaming and sobbing as well.'

'How did he get stuck?'

'He was scrambling across some wet rocks quite a way out and he slipped. His foot is jammed between two huge rocks. He can't pull it free. People have tried pulling him out but he's stuck fast.'

'OK,' I said. 'And the tide is coming in?'

'It'll be high tide soon. The poor bugger will be underwater at high tide. And there's a storm beginning to blow. The sea is getting rougher. Come as quickly as you can, doctor.'

'Where are you now?' I asked him.

'I'm at the Hunters Inn,' replied Bertram. 'I had to run all the way. Well, as much of it as I could.' He paused for a moment to get his breath. 'It's damned near done me in.'

The Hunters Inn is a wonderfully quaint, and rather gothic, Victorian building. It is now a popular pub and hotel which has for years been a magnet for tourists looking for a base from which to explore Exmoor and the North Devon Coast.

'I'll be there in at Hunter's Inn in 10 or 15 minutes,' I told him. 'Find someone with a motorbike who can take me down to the cove.'

'They don't allow motorbikes on the footpath,' said Bertram.

To me it seemed an unexpectedly silly thing to say. Under the circumstances, the rules didn't seem terribly important.

Suddenly, unexpectedly, Bertram started to cry. 'It's heart breaking to hear him. I don't think he can possibly have more than an hour at the very most.'

'See if you can find a motorbike. I'll be there as soon as I can.'

I picked up my black bag, went to the surgical supplies cupboard behind my desk and threw in some additional supplies – including a couple of scalpels, some extra suture materials and a couple of additional vials of morphine. As I did so, I shouted for Patsy.

'Please ring Patchy,' I asked her. 'Beg him to drop what he's doing and meet me at the Hunter's Inn, the pub at the start of the path down to Heddon's Mouth. If you can't get hold of Patchy find someone, anyone, with a motorbike and ask them to meet me there. A bloke is stuck in the rocks and I need to get down to the cove as quickly as possible.'

Patchy Fogg has a specially adapted motorbike, suitable for driving across quite rough and rocky terrain. He used it to very good effect when we were looking for Hamilton Murray on the North Devon Cliffs. I still believe that Patchy and his motorbike helped save Hamilton's life.

I kissed her, picked up my supplemented bag, took one last look at the surgical supplies cupboard to make sure there wasn't anything else I might need, and then ran out to the car. On the way to the car, I dashed into the garage and added another item to my drug bag. I looked up at the sky. It had suddenly occurred to me that maybe it would be possible to arrange for a helicopter to hover over Heddon's Mouth and help lift the poor guy to safety. But one look at the sky, and the storm already building up, and I knew that there was no chance of a rescue helicopter being able to help.

My heart was racing as I drove to down to Heddon's Mouth.

It seemed clear that neither the ambulance nor the fire service could possibly get to the man in time to be of any use.

It also seemed very clear that if the man's foot was stuck fast then I might have to amputate if his life was going to be saved. I had seen a leg amputated. But just once; when I'd been studying orthopaedics at medical school. But that had been some years ago. It had been a neat, below the knee amputation, performed in the sterile conditions of an operating theatre. If I had to amputate this poor man's foot, I would have to do so in awful conditions. But maybe we would be able to pull him free of the rocks. The storm was getting heavier by the minute and the sky was now nearly black. Although it was still afternoon I had to switch on the car's headlights.

I drove as fast I dared, hoping and praying that I wouldn't come across any other vehicles in the lanes. And God must have been listening because I didn't see any cars, lorries, coaches or, worst of all, any tractors or cars towing caravans.

The only delay occurred as I drove up a short hill leading from a lane in Bilbury to the road which winds down to Heddon's Mouth.

I found myself behind a cyclist, his machine weighed down with saddlebags, who steadfastly refused to move from the centre of the road as he pedalled merrily along, quite selfishly.

I tooted.

He ignored me.

I tooted again.

He just continued on his way, meandering from one side of the road to the other as he struggled to ride up the hill.

I tooted again.

By now I could feel my heart banging in my chest and my blood pressure starting to rise. I knew that every minute, every second, could make the difference between saving this man from the worst imaginable sort of death. Even if I couldn't save his life, I could at least give him an injection of something to put him to sleep.

All I could think of was this poor fellow, stuck fast in the rocks, watching each new wave reach higher. And his family were watching.

The damned cyclist still continued to ignore my tooting. He was now travelling at a slow walking pace.

Suddenly, I slammed on the brakes, leapt out of the car, pulled on the handbrake and ran up the hill until I was in front of the cyclist.

He was a man in his 40s; red-faced and now rather breathless.

'Please pull over to the side of the road and let me through,' I begged him.

He just stared at me.

He was travelling so slowly that I was able to stand in front of him and grab his handlebars. I held his bicycle. 'I'm a doctor,' I told him. 'There's a man trapped in the rocks and I need to get to him quickly. Please park your bicycle by the side of the road and let me come past.'

The man mumbled something rude and ungracious and then reluctantly and very slowly moved his machine to the side of the road.

I ran back to the car, jumped in, started up and drove past him.

Four minutes later, I slid into the car park at the inland end of the trail to Heddon's Mouth. Bertram, who was waiting there, rushed over to the car as I opened the door.

'Thank heavens you're here, doctor! What took you so long?'

'Did you find anyone with a motorbike?' I asked him.

'No,' said Bertram. 'But the man from the National Trust heard me asking and he told me what I told you: that motorbikes aren't allowed on the path down to the sea.'

'Did you tell him why I need to get there quickly?'

'Yes, but he said that's the rule. No bicycles or motorcycles on the path.'

A bearded fellow who looked to be in his late sixties or early seventies, wearing a tweed sports jacket and horn-rimmed spectacles, marched over to me. It seemed as though it were a day on which I was destined to have problems with men with beards.

'Motorbikes aren't allowed on the path down to the cove,' he said firmly and pompously.

Just then, Patchy screamed into the car park on his trails bike.

I picked my bag out of the car, locked the car and hurried over to him, ignoring the man from the National Trust.

'Thank heavens you're here!' I said. I rapidly explained the situation. 'If I walk it'll take me at least 30 minutes to get down to the sea. If you take me down there on the back of your bike we'll be there in a few minutes.'

'Motorbikes aren't allowed on the path!' said the elderly gentleman from the National Trust, shouting to make himself heard about the roar of Patchy's motorbike. He stood in front of us to block our way.

'Hop on,' said Patchy.

I climbed on, clutching my bag, and Patchy swung round the human obstacle and sped off with me clinging to the back of the bike for dear life.

Somewhere behind me, I could hear the man from the National Trust shouting at us. He seemed to be repeating his mantra that motorbikes weren't allowed on the footpath down to Heddon's Mouth. And I think he was threatening to call the police.

Patchy got me to the cove in less than five minutes.

It was the scariest and bumpiest and most uncomfortable journey of my life. There were dozens of people on the path, most of whom seemed quite oblivious of the fact that a man was stuck in the rocks just a short distance away. Patchy kept his finger on his horn and drove brilliantly, always giving walkers plenty of room and slowing down appropriately whenever we came across children or elderly walkers.

I was carrying a black medical bag and I would have thought it would have been obvious that we weren't joy-riding, but many of the people we whizzed past shouted angrily.

One young man grabbed my jacket and nearly pulled me off the bike; fortunately, the pocket he managed to catch hold of simply ripped free of the coat.

As we approached the sea, the sky seemed to grow steadily darker. The rain was now lashing down and the sky was split by flashes of lightning.

Without doubt, it was an afternoon to be tucked up with a log fire and a plateful of hot, buttered crumpets.

I assumed that the people we had passed on the path had been caught out by the sudden change in the weather. An hour or so earlier the sky had been blue and the sun had been shining. That fine weather was now but a distant memory.

When we finally reached the cove and I climbed down from the bike, I was shaking. I stood unsteadily for a moment or two. There were a dozen or so people standing around. None of them was doing anything. They were just looking out to sea. I could vaguely make out some figures on the distant rocks.

A woman in her late 20s or 30s was screaming and sobbing. Two children with her were sobbing quietly. One was a boy, one was a girl. The boy looked to be about six or seven-years-old. The girl was a year or two younger. A couple of older women were trying, in vain, to comfort the woman and her children.

The sea was wild and, driven by the wind, it was crashing onto the rocks with great ferocity. Above the sound of the sea and the rain and the wind, I could hear a man screaming.

From time to time, the black sky would be lit by flashes of lightning. It was a storm of biblical proportions; truly a tempest.

'Are you the doctor?' asked an ashen-faced man in a T-shirt and a pair of ragged shorts. I guessed from the colour of his limbs that underneath the pallor, a healthy suntan probably lay hidden.

I confirmed that I was indeed the doctor they'd been waiting for.

'He's over here,' said the ashen-faced man. 'Follow me and I'll take you to him. I know the best way to get to him.' He scrambled up onto a rock and began to make his way out towards the sea.

'I'll wait here,' said Patchy. 'If you need me to fetch anyone or organise any help just come and tell me, or send someone to let me know.'

I promised him that I would, and I set off after the pale-faced man. The rocks were wet and slippery and because I only had one hand free, I had difficulty keeping up with him.

After a few minutes of struggling across the rocks I could, at last, clearly see the man who was stuck. He looked to be in his early 30s. He was naked from the waist up and I could see, through the water, that he was wearing a pair of blue jeans. I couldn't see either of his legs below the knees. The water was well above his waist. I didn't know how fast the tide might come in but I knew from experience that in some of these small coves, when the weather is bad, the sea seems to come in very quickly.

The trapped man was alternately shouting and crying. Occasionally, he started to thrash around as though trying in vain to free himself. I'm not surprised. I doubt if anyone could have faced almost certain death in such awful, blood-curdling circumstances with any equanimity.

There were two men standing on the rocks nearby. One was tall and was, incongruously, wearing a light blue suit which was now soaked, ruined and sticking to him while the other man, much shorter and tubbier, was wearing shorts and a yellow anorak.

A third man, a youth really because he was no more than 19 or 20-years-old, was sitting on a rock next to the man who was stuck. I didn't recognise any of the three. I assumed they were all holidaymakers who were on the beach, or nearby, when the man got stuck. Locals don't tend to go down to Heddon's Mouth very much. The beach is very small, there's no fishing or surfing, it's a long walk and the place is usually crowded with tourists.

The tide was now so high, and the sea so rough, that when each new wave came crashing in the spray covered us all.

'I've got the doctor!' shouted my guide. The three men all looked in my direction.

The man who was trapped half turned 'Come and get me out,' he shouted. 'I'm going to drown.'

I bent down next to him and put my black bag down on a flattish piece of rock. The tide was now so high that the man's trapped right foot and lower leg were all under water. As I bent down to feel for his foot, to try to work out how badly he was stuck, a new wave arrived and crashed over us all. Not having had time to turn my face away I found myself with a mouth full of sea water. I spat the water out, and rubbed the salty water from my eyes.

'What's your name?' I asked him.

'Jeffrey,' he replied. 'Jeffrey Deacon.'

'Is it OK if I call you Jeffrey?'

'Yes.'

'I'm the doctor,' I told him. I told him my name. 'You're going to be fine. Can you move your foot?'

I tried to keep my voice as calm as I could, though I had to shout to make myself heard above the sound of the wind and the rain and the sea.

It isn't easy to sound calm when you're shouting.

Heddon's Mouth is a beautiful, quiet, peaceful spot on a calm day but when the weather turns bad it can, like much of the North Devon coast, be a truly inhospitable place.

Jeffrey nodded. He had stopped screaming and shouting. His eyes were red with crying.

I reached down into the sea water, felt his shin and then his ankle. I could not feel anything underneath his ankle. His foot had slipped down between two huge rocks and was now invisible. The gap between the rocks was so narrow that I definitely couldn't reach through to touch his foot.

Another huge wave crashed over us, soaking us again.

Out of the corner of my eye, I saw my black bag pushed off the rock where I had placed it. I just managed to grab it before it disappeared. I asked one of the men to hold it for me.

'Do something!' shouted the trapped man. 'I'm going to die.'

'You're not going to die,' I told him. 'You're definitely not going to die.'

He looked at me. There was a faint glimmer of hope in his eyes. But the hope did not last. 'You're lying!' he suddenly shouted. He made another effort to move himself but he was well and truly jammed. 'You know I'm going to die! You're going to let me die.'

I looked down into the water at his free leg to see what sort of footwear he was wearing. He had a fairly thin slip-on deck shoe. I was hoping that he might have been wearing a boot that might slip off. But the deck shoe on his trapped foot could not possibly make any difference.

Another huge wave crashed over us. The wind was getting stronger. The rain was now lashing down with ever greater fury. I was soaked to the skin and wondered momentarily why I had come out without any waterproofs. The sea level was rising every time another wave came in. The water was now up to the man's chest. I remember thinking that even if we got him free we would have to carry him all the way up Heddon's Valley. I remember wondering if a boat could come and take him to Barnstaple. That was my craziest thought. There was no chance whatsoever of any boat approaching the rocks in that weather. When you're desperate you have some daft ideas, don't you? Well, I do anyway.

'I'm not going to let you die,' I promised him and I damned well meant it.

I took my bag off the man who was holding it, opened it and took out a vial of morphine. It was raining so hard that within seconds, the inside of my bag was soaked and there was a growing puddle in the bottom. I don't think I've ever seen or felt such rain.

'I'm going to give you something to numb the pain,' I told him. He looked at me, puzzled. 'I'm not really in pain,' he said. I didn't tell him but I knew he was going to be and that whatever happened he would need the injection. I gave my bag to the short, tubby man in the yellow anorak and asked him to hold it for me. I found a vein in the trapped man's arm, swabbed it with a little cotton wool swab soaked in alcohol and wondered, not for the first time in my life, at the way we find ourselves sticking to our habits, however inappropriate the circumstances might be. I then injected a good dose of morphine.

I was giving him the morphine not to abolish any pain at that moment but to control the pain he was going to have in the not very distant future. I was also trying to put him to sleep for a while so that we could do whatever we needed to do to free him from the rocks.

'Are you putting him to sleep, doctor?' asked the tubby fellow who was holding my black bag. I suddenly noticed that he had enough chin for two people. It was an utterly irrelevant observation but I can remember his chin more than I can remember anything else about him. He hadn't shaved for a while and he reminded me of a cartoon character. It is strange how our minds latch onto minor irrelevancies. I have noticed that we often remember truly significant events by the smallest thing; a chance observation, an unusual smell, a startling sound.

'Just for a while,' I murmured.

'Poor devil,' muttered another one of the men, the tall one in the suit. I looked up. He crossed himself and I realised that he thought I had just killed the man so that he wouldn't have to die of drowning. The words 'putting to sleep' are widely used by vets when they euthanize animals.

'I've just sedated him so that we can get him out without causing him too much pain,' I explained. I was rather cross that they would think I would abandon the man's life so easily. I shivered and realised that I was very, very cold. Even today, years later, I can still feel that damned cold. It was a combination of the wind, the rain, the crashing sea and the fear.

'Let's try pulling him out,' I said. I looked round. My pale-faced guide had disappeared, gone back to the beach. 'There are four of us. Two to each arm and we just pull as hard as we can.'

'We tried pulling but he's jammed fast,' said the man in the suit.

'Of course you did,' I said. 'But he was fully conscious then and that probably stopped you pulling as hard as you can. Let's hold him and pull.' Another wave crashed over us.

The youth and the tubby man took his right arm and shoulder. And I and the man in a suit took his left arm and shoulder. I had to hold my black bag with my free arm so that it didn't get washed away.

'If we pull too hard we might pull off his foot,' said one of the men nervously. 'We shouldn't pull too hard.'

'If we can't pull him free I'm going to have to cut his foot off,' I thought. 'So it doesn't make much difference does it?' I didn't say this.

'We won't pull his foot off,' I assured them all.

I thought, but didn't say, that if we were going to save Mr Deacon from drowning then the whole business was going to be messy.'

We pulled. Oh how we pulled.

The main problem was that it was terribly difficult to get our footing on the slippery rocks. They were covered with seaweed and constantly being drenched with new clouds of spray and rain. Only the limpets and other shelled creatures clinging to the rocks helped to give our feet any traction.

We pulled so hard I thought we would dislocate Jeffrey Deacon's shoulders. But his foot was so tight that we could not pull it free. It occurred to me that the foot must have become swollen with all the pulling. I thought that maybe we could have pulled him out if we'd had ropes and some sort of hoist.

'Let's try again!' I told the others.

It did not seem possible that we could not pull Jeffrey's foot out from between the rocks. I knew that we would probably damage the skin and soft tissues, almost certainly damage the joint and possibly break a bone, but the alternative was much, much worse.

But we couldn't budge the trapped man.

'It's no good,' said the man in a suit. I didn't know his name. I didn't know any of their names. They were all brave to be out there on the rocks. The sea was very rough and the rain was lashing down. 'He's stuck fast. Give him a big injection, doctor. We're not going to be able to get him free. You've done your best.'

The water was now up to the top of the trapped man's chest. When a wave came in the spray reached over his head. In a few minutes time the man would be drowned and we would have to stand there and watch it happen.

'Hold him tight and pull him as upright as you can,' I told them. I opened my black bag and took out a scalpel, a strong cord and the hacksaw I'd taken from the garage. 'I'm going to have to amputate his foot.'

I suddenly realised that in my hurry, I hadn't brought a spare hacksaw blade with me. I hoped the blade that was in the saw would be strong enough to do the job. I then handed my black medical bag to one of the men and asked him to hold it for me. The rock upon which I had previously stood the bag was now under water. It was a perfect storm; a concatenation of difficult circumstances.

When he heard what I planned to do, the tubby fellow turned away and was sick.

'Should we ask his permission?' asked one of the men. I didn't know which one of them it was.

'He's unconscious,' I pointed out.

'We could ask his wife for permission,' he pointed out.

'I'm not sure whether a wife can give permission for a doctor to remove her husband's foot,' I said. 'But more importantly, by the time you've got back to the beach and asked her it will be too late to do anything.'

The sea now seemed to be rising even faster. The wind had whipped up the waves. When I looked out to sea, I could see that the breakers coming in looked to be seven or eight feet tall. Even at rest, the sea was now at the level of the trapped man's chin. I reckoned we only had another two or three minutes before he drowned. I had just two or three minutes to remove his trapped foot.

I rubbed the salt water out of my eyes with my sleeve, reached down into the water and felt for the lowest part of the man's leg. I then used the cord to tie a tourniquet around the man's leg, as low down as I could reach but allowing me room to cut through the leg.

I knew that when I cut through his leg there would be a good deal of bleeding. I needed to minimise the amount of blood loss. And I needed to work fast.

When I was a young hospital doctor, there was a surgeon who could perform amputations in world record time but not even he had been as fast as surgeons 100 years ago.

I remembered reading that in the 19th century, before anaesthesia had been invented, surgeons used to be able to perform amputations in seconds. One surgeon is said to have taken off a patient's arm while a colleague turned round to take a pinch of snuff. A Scottish surgeon called Robert Liston was timed at 33 seconds for an operation to remove a patient's leg at the thigh. Unfortunately, he was so fast that his assistant could not get his fingers out of the way in time. In addition to the patient's leg, three of the assistant's fingers succumbed to the saw and ended up in the waste bucket. Surgeons had to work fast if their patient was going to have a chance of surviving.

All this went through my mind in a flash.

Now, years later, I can still remember all these thoughts; slowed down in the way that the mind sometimes slows things down when we remember a bad accident.

As I tied the tourniquet, I called out to the young man and asked him to go back to the shoreline and to gather as many able bodied men and women he could find. I had to shout and repeat myself to make myself heard and understood.

'Tell them we're going to need people to carry Mr Deacon up to the road,' I told him. 'And find the man with the motorbike. His name is Patchy Fogg. Ask him to go back to the Hunter's Inn and to use their telephone to ring the ambulance people. We need an ambulance waiting at Hunter's Inn. If the ambulance people can't get here quickly then find someone with an estate car, a van or a small lorry. They'll need to take Mr Deacon to the hospital in Barnstaple.'

The young man nodded. I made him repeat what I'd told him. Then he hurried off.

I really didn't want him around when I cut off Mr Deacon's foot. I knew it was likely to be a sight likely to give birth to a hundred nightmares.

Cutting through bone isn't easy at the best of times.

Orthopaedic surgeons, who cut through bones and joints for a living, tend to be big beefy fellows. But cutting through bone you cannot see, when it is a few feet under water is considerably more difficult than cutting through bone in a nice, neat, aseptic operating theatre. And when the sea is crashing around and on top of you, the tide is coming in and the wind and the rain seem determined to wash you away, then it is, believe me, immeasurably more difficult.

And, of course, it was all made considerably more difficult by the fact that I had never, ever amputated a foot before. That was just a small, extra complication to add to all the others.

I took the hacksaw in my hand, crouched and reached down into the sea as far as I could stretch. I couldn't reach far enough down. The tide was coming in horrifically fast and I couldn't reach down to the man's ankle. I took a deep breath and put my head down under the water. It was freezing cold. I don't think I had ever been so cold, so scared and so anxious. I was now performing my first amputation and I was doing it under water, quite unable to see what I was doing.

I couldn't see anything but I could now feel the bottom of Jeffrey's leg, where it disappeared between the rocks.

I reached as far as I could and then used the hacksaw to cut through his jeans, his skin, his soft tissues and finally his bone. I worked frantically, against the clock. Sawing through his jeans wasn't easy. Sawing through his leg was brutally difficult. Butchers who chop up animal carcasses use nice sharp hatchets and knives and need a lot of force if they're going to chop through bone.

When I lifted my head to take another breath, I heard the man who had been sick say that we were all going to drown and he was going back to the beach. He sounded as if he were a thousand miles away. I think he was crying.

Most people really don't realise how hard it is to cut through bone.

If your dog finds an old bone sometime, try cutting through it with a saw. You'll be amazed at how difficult it is. Bone is a very hard substance.

I put my head back into the water, cut a little more, raised my head to take another breath, then went back under the water, trying to find where I'd started cutting so that I could carry on in the same spot.

By the time I'd finished cutting and Jeffrey Deacon was free from the rocks, I was utterly exhausted and I was nearly drowned myself. I had swallowed far more sea water than is good for anyone.

'He's free,' I gasped, to the remaining two men, as I harnessed my last remaining strength and dragged Jeffrey Deacon free of the gap between the two rocks, terrified he would slip and slide back into the crack where his detached foot now remained.

I looked down into the water, wondering if I could see his foot and ankle. But I couldn't, of course. I couldn't see anything but water. I heard thunder crashing. It sounded close. I'd missed the lightning.

'Help me carry him to the beach. Don't try and rush it.'

I didn't want us dropping him and cracking open his skull on a rock. And I didn't want one of us sliding between two slippery, seaweed covered rocks and getting stuck. That thought went through my mind. Later, I would have a recurring nightmare in which all of us were stuck in the rocks with huge, 20-foot high waves bearing down on us.

Before we began to carry him to comparative safety, I sat for a couple of moments on a barnacle encrusted rock and tried to get my breath back.

The life of a country GP sometimes seems stranger than fiction.

A huge wave crashed over us all and the man who was holding my black bag let go of it.

I watched in horror as the bag disappeared into the sea. I prayed Mr Deacon didn't wake up because now I had no more morphine to give him and nothing with which to give it to him. This rescue was now beyond being a nightmare.

I'd got the trapped man free of the rocks and I'd saved him from drowning. Now we had to get him all the way up the Haddon Valley and to a hospital as soon as possible.

And there was now something else; something more personal.

Deep down I knew that I would probably have to cope with the wrath of the man and his wife when they discovered that I'd had to remove his foot. It occurred to me that he might sue me. Would he have a case? Would others say I should have done things differently? It is always so much easier to make decisions when sitting, quietly in an air-conditioned courtroom than when facing a real life crisis in unbearable circumstances, with the clock ticking ever faster and ever louder. I could not think of anything I could have done differently. But would a judge think differently? I knew damned well that there would be a doctor somewhere who would, for a fat fee, be happy to pass judgement on what I had done, why I had done it and how I had done it.

Meanwhile, I was physically and mentally exhausted and we still had to drag and carry Mr Deacon to the beach. I could see people waving to us, beckoning to us. Two or three men started out across the rocks towards us, scrambling, sliding and falling but gradually getting closer.

Somehow, the three of us managed to carry and drag Mr Deacon across the rocks and to the shore. The men who had scrambled out to meet us helped enormously. The three of us were exhausted. Simply staying on the rocks, as the sea and the storm fought to wash us to our deaths, had taken an enormous amount of energy and will.

On the beach, the man's wife was waiting. She still had her children by her side. You might have thought that someone would have spotted that her husband had no foot, and would have taken the children away. But no one had done anything.

The woman was sobbing with relief. Then she saw her husband's bloody leg. And the children saw it too. The small boy saw it first. He told his sister. They were shouting and crying and pointing. The woman tried to get to her husband. We had to hold him up because he was unconscious and he couldn't stand.

'We have to hurry!' I shouted. 'We have to get him up the path to the car park. God willing there will be an ambulance waiting for us. But we have to get him there quickly.'

The tourniquet I'd tied was preventing serious blood loss but there was still blood seeping out from the ugly wound I'd made.

I asked two of the men to hold him upright while I knelt down and unfastened the tourniquet for a moment, to let some blood into the remaining tissue, to keep it alive and healthy.

I saw a large pram that someone had pushed down the path and wondered if we could use it to wheel Mr Deacon to the ambulance. I decided it would be more trouble than it was worth. I looked around and counted. There were nine able-bodied men there. 'Carry him in relays,' I shouted. 'A couple of hundred yards at a time.'

'What have you done to him?' demanded Mrs Deacon. She was a big, tough, brawny woman who looked as if she could have hefted hundred weight coal sacks for a living. She stuck her face a foot from mine. She had long, black hair which was plastered to her head. Her dress was soaked. She had been crying endlessly. She was distraught and I understood. 'You've made him into a cripple!' she shouted at me. I could only just hear her above the sound of the wind and the rain. 'You bastard! What have you done to him? What have you done to him?' She lashed out at me and caught me quite a painful blow on the arm.

'I had no choice,' I told her. 'He was trapped. He would have drowned.'

'You could have pulled him out!'

'We tried but we couldn't. He was stuck fast. He would have died.'

'You should have waited!'

'I couldn't wait!' I told her.

'I told him not to go scrambling over those rocks,' she said, sobbing.

Mrs Deacon needed support and help but I didn't have the time and this was not the place. I turned away to the men who were still waiting. 'Get moving!' I told them urgently. 'We have to get him to the ambulance.'

We moved as a convoy.

I led the way, followed by the men who were carrying Mr Deacon. Mrs Deacon hurried along beside them, dragging her children. She kept getting in the way and slowing them down. I could totally understand her concern, anguish, agony and desperation but she was making things worse for her husband who was, in any case, still unconscious. The men who weren't actually carrying followed behind.

Half way along the path, I heard a motorbike and Patchy appeared through the darkness and the rain.

'There's no ambulance yet but I've got a guy with a Dormobile ready and waiting to take your patient to the hospital,' said Patchy. 'With any luck the ambulance will be waiting by the time you get there.'

And, thank God, it was.

I told the ambulance men how much morphine I'd given so that they could tell the doctors in Barnstaple. Mrs Deacon insisted on climbing into the back of the ambulance with her husband. Naturally, she insisted on taking the children with her. The ambulance men weren't happy but they couldn't keep her out. I decided that Mr Deacon no longer needed me and, given Mrs Deacon's anger, that it would be best if I stayed behind.

'Looks like you've had a busy day,' said Patchy, as the ambulance sped off to the hospital in Barnstaple.

I just looked at him and shook my head in dismay and weariness. I was mentally and physically exhausted. I couldn't help but hope that there were no more calls for a while. I looked at my watch. I was nearly an hour late for the evening surgery. I hoped that the non-urgent patients would have gone home, to return tomorrow.

I remember looking around for my drug bag and realising it had been lost at sea. I'd have to get another. And there was quite a good deal of expensive equipment to replace too.

I thanked Patchy, climbed into the Rolls and drove slowly home to Bilbury Grange. I was confident that Mr Deacon would now live. He would obviously have to come to terms with having lost his foot and I knew there would be difficult times ahead for him and his family. But he would be alive.

Would Mrs Deacon still be angry in the morning? Would she report me to the General Medical Council? Would she want to sue me?

The drive home, though only a couple of miles or so, seemed endless.

When I got back to Bilbury Grange I pretty well fell out of the car.

'There are just six patients still waiting for you,' said Patsy, throwing a blanket around me for I was starting to shiver. 'Do you want me to ask them to wait while you have a hot bath or do you want to see if you can deal with them now, and then have a hot bath?'

I said I'd try to deal with the evening surgery straight away. Patsy made me a hot coffee, laced with whisky. I sat in the surgery, dripping wet and with a huge blanket thrown around my shoulders.

I must have broken all records for conducting a surgery. There were no urgent or serious problems and I finished the entire evening's work in under ten minutes.

And then I collapsed into a warm bath with a glass of hot whisky to keep me company. There I stayed, repeatedly topping up with hot water until the water went so cold that topping it up with hot would have resulted in the bath overflowing. I wanted to relax but I couldn't. I kept asking myself if I could have done anything differently. Was there anything that I could have done to save the man's foot? Could I have somehow rescued the amputated foot in the hope that surgeons might be able to sew it back on?

In the end I knew, just knew, that I couldn't think of anything I could have done that would have saved his foot. And I was satisfied that I could not possibly have rescued the amputated foot.

But I was still worried about the consequences.

No doctor wants angry patients or relatives attacking him.

Would the Deacons attack me? The rescue was bound to attract some publicity. Would the Deacons vilify me in public? Would they sue me? The questions kept recurring; going round and round in my mind.

I dressed and went back downstairs. Patsy had lit a roaring log fire.

We sat in front of the fire and ate egg and chips. There is much comfort to be had from watching a log fire crackle and spit. There is comfort for the eyes and for the ears. And I enjoy the smell of a log fire, too.

Afterwards, I talked to Patsy about what had happened. I told her how I'd had to cut off a man's foot while he was trapped and about to drown. I told her how absolutely terrified I had been and how I had, for quite a while, been convinced that the man was going to drown. I told her of the bravery of the strangers who had stayed with him on the rocks.

I told her, in the end, that whether I had done well or badly, I knew I'd done the best I could. And you can never do more than that.

We had one nasty moment that evening.

At about 9.00 pm, a reporter telephoned and asked if I'd heard that the Deacons were going to sue me for damages.

But it turned out to be a hoax. The reporter had merely been trying to stir up a story.

The men who had stayed with me on the rocks all confirmed that if I had not amputated Mr Deacon's foot then he would have died.

They said kind things which I much appreciated.

And in the end, the Deacons were very kind, gracious, forgiving and, yes, grateful. They both understood that if I had not amputated then Mr Deacon would have died. And they considered the loss of a foot a relatively small price to pay for life.

I was relieved and delighted when the rescue didn't get much coverage in the media. It had apparently been a busy news day. A celebrity had said something controversial, a member of the Royal family had done something curious, a film star had been caught in an affair and there had been a political row in Westminster.

A storm in Devon, and the near drowning of a man caught in the rocks, could not compete with these big news stories. Mr Deacon's brush with death made just a few inches in the local papers. There were no cameras there and so there was no coverage on television.

A week afterwards, a delivery van turned up and the driver presented me with a parcel and asked me to sign for it.

The parcel contained a new medical bag. It was a 'thank you' from the Deacons who had somehow heard that I'd lost my previous black bag during the rescue.

I've still got the bag.

It is one of my most treasured possessions.

And finally…
I hope you have enjoyed this book about my adventures in Bilbury. If you did so then it would mean a great deal to me if you would spare a moment to write a short review.
Thank you
Vernon Coleman

Appendix 1
My Favourite Latin Phrases

Here is the list of Latin phrases which Esme Church compiled for me (as described in 'Cedric's Admirers').

Aegrescit medendo – the remedy makes things worse
Aequam servare mentem – to keep a calm mind and, as Kipling suggested, to treat success and disaster equally
Aut vincere aut mori – either conquer or die
Compos mentis – having control of one's own mind
De mortuis nil nisi bonum – say nothing but good of the dead
Diem perdidi – I have lost a day (Suetonius allegedly said this when once at dinner he remembered he had done nothing for anybody all that day)
Dum spiro, spero – while I breathe I hope, where there is life there is hope
Ex ovo omnia – every living thing comes from an egg (attributed to William Harvey, the discoverer of the human circulatory system)
Felix qui potuit rerum cognoscere causas – there is happiness for the man who is able to discover why things happen
Homo sum, humani nihil a me alienum puto – I am a man and there is no human problem which does not concern me
In articulo mortis – spoken at the point of death
Icundi acti labores – completed labours are pleasant – from Euripides who meant, I think, that it is good to look back on trials and hardships when one has come through them safely
Mens sibi conscia recti – knowing within oneself that one has done the right thing
Naturam expellas furca, tamen usque recurret – even though you drive out nature with a pitchfork, she will always return
Nescit vox missa reverti – a word once published cannot be recalled
Nullum magnum ingenium sine mixtura dementiae fuit – all great geniuses have some madness in them

Possunt quia posse videntur – they can because they think they can (the power of the mind)
Senex bis puer – the old man is twice a child (in old age)
Taedium vitae – weariness of life, extreme ennui
Venienti occurrite morbo – run to meet disease as it comes, don't wait for sickness to develop and get worse

Appendix 2
The Tilbury Gig and other Horse Drawn Conveyances

In 'Mrs Leeson's Leg', I described how Mrs Leeson drove around in a Tilbury gig. With the aid of Patchy Fogg and Mrs Leeson's groom/chauffeur, I have compiled a short dictionary describing the various types of carriage which were used in England in the 19th and 20th centuries.

Barouche: a four-seater carriage, half covered; the two front passengers face the two back ones

Brougham: a closed carriage with 2 or 4 wheels, pulled by one horse

Cabriolet: two wheeled carriage with an open hood pulled by one horse (usually offered for hire, hence the abbreviation 'cab' which is used to describe a taxi)

Chariot: originally a two wheeled vehicle drawn by horses and used in racing and warfare; more recently the term was sometimes used to describe a four wheeled open carriage with a coachman's seat at the front.

Clarence: a four-seater carriage

Curricle : a light two wheeler which was popular in the 18th century and which is the father of the Victorian dog cart (early dog carts were actually drawn by dogs)

Dennet: a light two-seater gig

Dicky: a folding outside seat, usually fixed at the back of a carriage and used by a servant

Fly: similar to phaeton, also called a rat

Four wheeler: a large hansom cab; also known as a 'growler'

Gig: a light two-seater carriage pulled by one horse

Hansom: known as the gondola of London; a hansom cab is a low, two wheeled cabriolet for two passengers. The driver sits behind his passengers and with the reins going over the top. Named after Joseph Hansom who was an English architect. He patented the design in 1834.

Landau: a four wheeled enclosed carriage which has a removable front cover and a back cover that can be raised or lowered. Named after the town of Landau in Germany, where it was first produced. Popularly used by monarchs and others who need to be seen by the public but who need some protection lest the weather turn bad.

Phaeton: a four wheeled pleasure carriage which has all the seats facing forward

Rumble: a dicky seat for less regarded passengers or servants (when John Brown rode with Queen Victoria in her Sociable he took the rumble seat)

Sociable: a rather genteel phaeton with four wheels and a collapsible hood. The two main seats face front and there is a pull out stool facing them. A 'sociable' was used by Queen Victoria when not on State business and came to be known as a Victoria

Stanhope: a light one-seater open carriage with two or four wheels; named after Fitzroy Stanhope who was an English clergyman.

Tilbury gig: a light two-seater, pulled by a single horse

Trap: a light, simply made, two-wheeled carriage which is usually pulled by a small horse or pony

Victoria: see 'sociable'

Appendix 3
Plants Named After Parts of the Human Body

During one conversation in the Duck and Puddle (described in 'Caleb's Ankle'), Thumper, Patchy and I spent some time chatting to a local man called Caleb Theodore.

Caleb told us that a surprising number of plants are named after parts of the human body.

With his help, I compiled this list. All these plants are real!

Black maidenhair
Bladder campion
Bladderwort
Dead man's fingers
Eyesbright
Heartsease
Hounds tongue
Kidney vetch
Lady's tresses
Liverwort
Lords and ladies
Lungwort
Maidenhair
Miller's thumb
Naked ladies
Navelwort
Nipplewort
Old man's beard
Open arse
Prick madam
Priests ballocks (sic)
Shitabed
Skullcap
Stinking willy

Finally, but certainly not least, I must give an honourable mention to a plant which doesn't really fit on this list but which has, in my view, the best name ever given to a plant: the 'welcome-home-husband-though-never-so-drunk'.

Caleb tells me that the name is popularly used to describe sempervivum tectorum (apparently known to its chums as the common houseleek and to its posher chums as sedum acre) which is a flowering plant found on high ground in southern Europe.

Appendix 4
Types of Auction

In 'The Bathroom Cabinet' I mentioned a 'time auction'. With the aid of Patchy Fogg I have compiled a list of the most popular types of auction.

Ordinary English auction: the auctioneer invites bids and the bidders push up the prices bit by bit.
A Dutch auction: this type of auction works in reverse. The auctioneer starts at a high price and the price falls until a bidder says he'll pay that price.
Paper or silent auction: the auctioneer announces a minimum price and the bidders write down their bids and the highest wins.
Ring auction: dealers agree not to bid. One of them buys the item. They then all meet and have the auction between themselves.
Market auction: bidders bid on a bunch of similar items and can take as many items as they like at that price.
Time auction: the bidding stops at a pre-arranged time. This type of auction is invariably pretty chaotic. The French have a version which is commonly used when selling wine. The auctioneer lights a candle and bidders can bid for as long as the candle remains alight. When the candle goes out, the highest bidder gets the item.

Appendix 5
D is for Diarrhoea, F is for Flatulence, P is for Piles

Air traffic controllers, policemen and telephone operators all use an official alphabet aid which includes such items as 'W for whisky' and 'G for golf'. The idea is to avoid misunderstandings. But the official alphabet aid (created by NATO) is quite boring so I have created a less po-faced alternative on a medical theme. The list was created after the conversation I described in 'The Bathroom Cabinet'.

A for Abscess
B for Breast
C for Cramp
D for Diarrhoea
E for Earache
F for Flatulence
G for Gall stones
H for Hernia
I for Indigestion
J for Jaundice
K for Kidneys
L for Liver
M for Muscles
N for Nipple
O for Ointment
P for Piles
Q for Quinsy
R for Ringworm
S for Sphincter
T for Tonsils
U for Uterus
V for Verucca
W for Waterworks
X for X-ray

Y for Yellow-fever
Z for Zit

I have donated this new alphabetical aid free of charge to the English speaking world.

Please pass it on to your friends, neighbours and colleagues so that they can stop using the old, banned, boring system and ensure that they are using the up-to-date medical alphabet nomenclature.

And finally (again)...
I hope you have enjoyed this book about Bilbury and the people who live in and visit the village. If you did so, then I would be very grateful if you would spare a moment to write a short review. This is the 11th book in the series entitled The Young Country Doctor.
Thank you
Vernon Coleman

Printed in Great Britain
by Amazon